"Claim the Prosperity that is your Birthright!"

Accept Your Abundance!

Why You Are Supposed To Be Wealthy

By Randy Gage

Gage, Randy.
   Accept your abundance! : why you are supposed to be
   wealthy / by Randy Gage. — 1st ed.
   p. cm.
   "Claim the prosperity that is your birthright!"
   LCCN 2003102890
   ISBN 097155787X

   1. Success—Psychological aspects. 2. Self-actualization
(Psychology) 3. Conduct of life. I. Title.

BF637.S8G34 2003   158.1
                              QBI33-1266

"Accept Your Abundance" is part of a five-book series on Prosperity.

101 Keys to Your Prosperity

Accept Your Abundance! Why You are supposed to be Wealthy

37 Secrets About Prosperity

The 7 Spiritual Laws of Prosperity and How to Manifest Them in Your Life

Prosperity Mind: How to Harness the Power of Thought

Published by:
Prime Concepts Publishing
A Division of Prime Concepts Group, Inc.
1807 S. Eisenhower Street
Wichita, Kansas 67209-2810 USA

Order Information:
To order more copies of this book, or to receive a complete catalog of other products by Randy Gage, contact:

Prime Concepts Group, Inc.
1-800-946-7804 or (316) 942-1111
or purchase online at:
www.RandyGage.com
www.Prosperity-Insights.com

Dedication

This book is dedicated to Coach Dennis Butler, because if anybody in the world deserves a dedication in a book, he is the guy!

Acknowledgements . . .

I would like to express my appreciation to the amazing Lornette Browne, who keeps me accepting my own abundance. And Lisa Jimenez, just because she is Lisa.

Introduction

Introductions are a good place to answer a question that authors get a lot. Namely, why did you write the book? So, here goes . . .

Almost everyone you meet will tell you they want to be healthy, happy, and rich. Yet very few of them have two out of three, and almost none of them have all three. So some years back, I started sharing what I learned about how to be prosperous. I'm a very rational, logical person, so I broke down the process, and explained it in a very rational, logical way. After a few years of this, I came to understand something quite extraordinary . . .

The problem for most people wasn't lack of knowledge. I could teach that pretty easily. The real issue was that they simply couldn't, or wouldn't, let themselves become prosperous. They actually sabotaged their prosperity, on a subconscious level.

They refused to accept their abundance. And nothing could be more tragic, than untapped potential, unfulfilled happiness, and unclaimed prosperity.

So that's why I wrote the book. I want you to have all the abundance that is your birthright.

Randy Gage
Key West, Florida
March 2003

Table of Contents

Chapter One:
Putting Yourself in the Prosperity Picture

Twice a year, I go on a Mastermind Retreat with the top-level members of my coaching program. At a Retreat in Costa Rica recently, I was working with an entrepreneur on growing his business. I came up with an idea that could generate $15 or $20 million a year in revenue, and had the potential for $30 million a year quite readily. At that time, he was probably only doing less than $300,000 a year.

You might think he jumped at the chance. You might think you would have too. But he didn't. And you might not have either . . .

As I sketched out the concept, I could see both him and his wife tuning out. It became obvious to the group and me that they simply were on overload. They had come expecting to learn how to make an extra $50,000, or maybe $250,000, but when I started talking millions, it just was simply too much for them to believe.

Now, to be fair, they didn't first perceive the situation that way . . .

They felt like they supported the idea. But they kept raising objections like the idea was difficult, needed more research, would take years to develop, etc. It was only when the entire group confronted them, that they accepted the possibility that they might be running from the idea because it was too prosperous for them to accept.

They left with the agreement that they would listen to my "Prosperity" audio album and work on their prosperity consciousness.

At the next Retreat, they both felt that they had worked through their prosperity issues and were willing to accept this bold, new plan I had for their business. So I asked the wife a very simple question . . .

I asked her how their lives would be different, if their business did $30 million in the next year. Her answer was quite fascinating . . .

She insisted that it would pretty much stay the same. She made a great point to confirm that her needs were basically met, and the only real difference was that she wouldn't have so much stress about paying bills.

I wanted more. I pressed her for tangible changes that would take place in her lifestyle. EVERYTHING she came up with had to do with helping someone else.

She would sponsor a Boy Scout camp, help out her parents, sponsor a school, etc. She didn't name one thing she would do for herself. I threw the question to her husband . . .

He started where she left off, but he got more specific. He mentioned the exact Boy Scout activities that they would sponsor, and suggested that he would hire a 24-hour caregiver for his sick father. Like his wife, he only mentioned doing things for other people. Absolutely nothing either of them suggested was for themselves. It was all about giving things to others.

So still I kept pressing . . .

After much searching, he finally suggested that they could get a cabin on the lake. This prompted his wife, who finally acknowledged that she would like a 4-wheel drive vehicle. I thought we were finally getting somewhere. Until she said the reason she wanted the new vehicle was so she could drive

even more boy scouts to the camp they would sponsor!
It became quite obvious that neither of them had even the
remotest idea of how their lives would be different with an
extra $30 million. And because they haven't foreseen this
possibility, they can't manifest it.

Trying to figure out the WHY . . .

I asked the people in my coaching program what they felt
had been holding them back over the years. They had
some intriguing insights. One student wrote, "I've accepted
for quite some time that I manifest my own difficulties. (I
understand this logically; I'm still working on accepting it in
my heart.) My question has been, not 'Why did this happen
to me?' but 'WHY have I manifested these problems?'"

"The classic 'fear of success?' I don't think so. I've
been healthy and successful, and I enjoyed it. Fear of
failure? Again, I don't think so. I don't enjoy failure, but I
don't fear it either. I recognize that it's a necessary part
of the process."

"Low self-esteem? That's certainly part of it. But I don't
feel that that's the underlying reason. And then, a few days
ago, a possibility hit me . . ."

We'll continue in a second with what this student came up
with. First, however, I want you to ask about YOU.

Do you recognize and accept that you bring your difficulties
upon yourself? Or are you still blaming fate, bad luck, the
economy, your ex-spouse, or the communist conspiracy?

And if you do accept this, what do you think is your 'Why?'

Here is what the student came up with. He writes, "I
manifested these challenges to give me challenges to

overcome! (I'm not saying that this is 'right' thinking or even 'sane', I'm just searching for reasons for my behavior.) "For much of my adult life, I've enjoyed being on the 'losing team,' and helping them to fight their way to the championship playoffs. Over and over, I've accepted challenges, just to prove to myself that I could meet the challenge head-on."

Now I think we're really on to something here. As I look back on my "dark years" (the first 30 years of my life!), I realize that I most definitely had a similar mindset.

Which takes us to the next big issue . . .

Namely—why would you, I, or anyone, want (or need) to overcome such challenges? Give that some real thought. Because the answer to that question, has the power to turn your life around in the snap of your fingers.

Please read that last sentence again.

Here's what else my students came up with. "I think I've dug this particular hole for myself, just so I could find a way to climb out of it! I'd like to say that it's because it enables me to learn and grow (that's the noble reason), but I think there may be more to it than that. I feel that there are some deeper issues at work, and when I can uncover them, I may no longer feel the need to manifest challenges in my life. I'd like that."

As well he should! As I look back on my own mindset in my lean years, I think I found it romantic to be the little guy fighting the forces of evil. I relished in the camaraderie of sharing all my victim experiences with all my victim friends. (Which is what I did on a daily basis.)

This topic generated a slew of responses on the website

from other students as well. One lady wrote, "Maybe I've tried to make things more difficult for myself so that I could give the impression that I was clever and skilled. I've always been a little suspicious when a job or a problem looked too easy to solve. 'Are they really easy or am I not looking at it right, not seeing the traps?' And here's what I did. I made it difficult so that I wouldn't be uncertain anymore, 'cause now it really was difficult! And everybody could see it!"

Does that strike a chord with you?

Another student mentions something similar. She says, "From when I was very young and until I began on this journey, I have been a Champion in creating challenges—or manifesting difficulties —for myself! I definitely think it goes back to how I was brought up, and a lack of self-worth, and also I believe I was born with fighter genes. So seeking challenges, creating some kind of chaos, or helping the losing team—was who I was, it was all something I was good at handling, and the admiration from others made me feel soooo good!"

Finally, another student writes, "I gloried in choosing what I perceived to be the harder path as though I seemed ennobled by suffering. It really brought me nothing but lots of angst and little else to show for it—maybe except for so-called battle scars I can regale the petty tyrants in my life with. It's as though this gave me an excuse to be mediocre because, really, I was building character (damn straight!) and testing my own sense of self-worth with every big problem I had managed to manifest in my life."

I saw this pattern repeated over and over, amongst all different ages, and types of students, from several dozen different countries. It is somehow comforting to think we manifest challenges because we love the challenge. And it's reassuring to think that we are building character; that we do this because it makes the ultimate victory sweeter, etc. But what if it isn't those things at all?

As I dug deeper into the research, I came up with another core motivation. I believe that manifesting difficult challenges is simply another way to hold on to being a victim! We create more challenges because it allows us to get sympathy from others; we have an excuse for failure; and we don't have to feel responsible for not succeeding. It's the ultimate cop-out.

It allows us to lie to ourselves. We figure that no one can say we didn't give it our best shot. We can say, "I gave it my all but I: didn't have the connections/was from the wrong side of the tracks/am the wrong color/don't have the education required." It is a built-in validation for a life of mediocrity.

But, here's the really good news. If you can create difficulty, strain, and suffering as evidenced by your past, what's to stop you from creating success, flow, and happiness in your life right NOW?

Getting Over the Need to be a Victim . . .

What do you have to do, to release the victim mentality forever? It's a very intriguing question. Because everyone would say that they are interested in losing the victim mentality. Everyone. But that wouldn't be the truth.

We know many people will hold on to, or manifest new challenges because it takes off pressure to perform. It gives them a ready-made excuse. This type of lack thinking can show up in many areas of your life...

I remember when I had a "bad back." Whenever I started a new relationship, the pattern was the same. I would wake up; start to get out of bed; and hold my lower back. My partner would ask something like, "What's the matter? Your back bothering you?"

"Yeah," I'd reply. "I've got a bad back." That would then start the discussion about ice packs, massages, hot tubs, surgery, and all the other treatments for back trouble. And affirm and own my "bad back" for the term of that relationship.

But what was it really?

It was my response to the emotional development I had at the time. Namely an inability to give or receive love. Like most of the people in my family, I didn't hug, express affection, or say "I love you" very much. After four years of therapy, I noticed something funny . . .

Once I developed the ability to express and accept love—I didn't have a bad back anymore! And I came to realize that I had manifested a bad back, serious allergy problems, and other health challenges because that's how I got attention and affection. What I perceived as love. Wow, what a wake-up call that was.

So why I am telling you all this?

To raise the critical question of how you see yourself. Have you seen your own success and prosperity already? Do you know what your life would look like if you were living your abundance? Or do you still see yourself as the noble underdog, fighting off challenge after challenge? It's worth some real reflection.

Chapter Two
Starring in Your Own Movie

So when I presented the business concept that could make them tens of millions of dollars, what was stopping the couple in my Mastermind group from embracing it? And could the same thing be holding you back?

Think about the goals you have for yourself. How big are they? More importantly, have you thought about exactly how that would play out in your life?

Let's suppose you say that you want to earn $2 million a year. Do you know what that really looks like for you? How much is that a month? What does the weekly paycheck look like? What's your tax bill? What kind of house would you live in? What car(s) would you be driving? How would that change the interaction you would have with those you love?

Or suppose your dream is to be a professional football player, or a concert pianist. What would your average day look like? What would you be doing?

The more you can really see your abundance, the more likely you are to attract it.

I have a friend named Richard Brooke, who runs a network marketing company, and frequently conducts workshops on vision. At his workshops, he mentions several interesting things that concern us here . . .

He was once at an event, and saw a booth where they made souvenir mockups of magazine covers. So he put himself on the cover of "SUCCESS" magazine. He had it framed and he kept it in his office by his desk, so he saw it every day.

About two years later, SUCCESS decided to do a cover story on the growth of Network Marketing. They wanted to put the president of Amway on the cover, but they were on a tight deadline, and he didn't return their call. So, they called Richard, did a photo shoot, and put him on the cover. To this day, he maintains that the reason that happened, is because he had that souvenir mockup in his office.

He saw himself as the cover subject for two years. So he attracted it to himself, because he was ready to accept his abundance!

One of the things that Richard has people do in his seminars is write a movie script of their perfect day. So for example, let's suppose your vision is to be the number one sales producer for the organization you work with. You write that movie.

So you might pick the day of the annual convention, where you will receive your award. Starting with waking up in the morning, you write out your day. So you might talk about the smell of coffee downstairs that you wake up to. Feel the breeze coming in the window, and hearing the dog bark with happiness when you come downstairs. You would describe the breakfast you ate, and the conversation you had with your partner.

You might mention the red Lamborghini with the leather seats that you drive to the hotel where the conference is being held, and the tumultuous ovation you receive, when you go on stage to get your award. The key here is that you involve all of your senses, and paint the picture as vividly as you can.

Stuff that would be minutiae in a real Hollywood script is very important to you. So don't hold back on any details. If you are having homemade strawberry jam with the cream cheese on your cinnamon raisin bagel for breakfast—write it down!

You want a compelling and thorough journaling of your perfect day—the day you want to manifest. You want to see it, hear it, taste it, smell it, touch it, and FEEL it. It is only when you experience prosperity in your mind and heart first, that you manifest it on the physical plane.

Don't show this script to anyone, except those who support and encourage you greatly. Many people in "the herd" will only be jealous and ridicule you. Share it only with those you can count on as Mastermind partners toward your success.

Keep this script in some place like your planner, briefcase, or purse, so you have it handy every day. When you're waiting in line at the grocery store, read a few paragraphs of your script instead of the tabloid headlines. When you get stressed out during your day and feel overwhelmed, close your door, take the phone off the hook for five minutes and read your script.

Your script will center you, calm you, and reinforce the positive programming in your subconscious mind. This is a very powerful tool for accepting your abundance.

Start writing yours today!

Chapter Three
The Danger of Lack Programming

So why might you not be accepting all the abundance that is meant for you?

Because you've been programmed that money is bad, rich people are evil, and it is spiritual to be poor. And this programming started when you were an infant.

I grew up watching TV shows like "Gilligan's Island," "MASH," and "The Beverly Hillbillies." All pretty silly, innocuous shows, right? Well let's analyze them from a prosperity standpoint.

Remember the millionaire on Gilligan's show? He had a pretentious name, and was always portrayed as a goofy rich person. Think how the banker and people with money were portrayed in the "Hillbillies." The Hillbillies were always presented as sensible, down-to-earth people, who were amused and bemused by the crazy way rich people acted.

MASH centered around the two good guys, and then there was always a bad guy, usually a rich guy who listened to Opera, and also had a pretentious name. I could go on, but you get the picture. I look back on it now, and I realize that I was probably programmed against rich people before I was ten years old!

What about you? If you grew up in a different time frame than me, think about the shows you watched. How were rich people portrayed? (Think about J.R. on "Dallas," all the conniving rich people on "Dynasty," and the way the media slants the stories about the ultra-rich people like Bill Gates, Ross Perot and Ted Turner.)

Do you realize that the average person watches 6 hours of TV per day? That equals 42 hours a week and 168 hours a month. So that means in one month, they watched approximately 6,720 commercials and accumulated seven full 24-hour days worth of mostly useless and often lack-centered information.

For every hour you were listening to the radio, you put even more commercials and useless information into your brain. If you just listened to the radio in your car, you might be subjected to 5 to 10 hours of status quo information per week, or 20 to 40 hours per month.

Newspapers and magazines add even more redundant information and advertising into your mind. Newspapers are full of information written by people who are not at all educated about the things they are reporting. They rely heavily upon slanting their articles in a way to draw out your emotional response to sell more newspapers.

It's certainly not getting better today. In fact, you can make the case that it is getting much worse.

Last year I made a prediction about a soon-to-be-released book, entitled "The Nanny Diaries." I guaranteed that it would be a monster hit. Which it was. How did I know it would be?

Because I read an advance review in the *USA Today,* and it was obvious that the book pandered to the basest lack and limitation programming of the masses. The very first sentence of the review stated, "Quite simply there is nothing more delectable than evidence that being very rich and very thin does not mean that one is happy."

That one sentence tells you everything you need to know about the role of the media in shaping your perception of success, happiness, and money. But there is plenty more.

The review and story are simply saturated with statements to promote lack consciousness. Here's a sampling:

" . . . perfectly captures the strange and pampered life of New York's elite as they skillfully evade raising their own offspring."

" . . . wonderfully sets up the world of very rich women who devote enormous energy to monitoring what their children eat but who never actually sit down with them."

"Just how does an intelligent, adult woman become someone whose whole sterile kingdom has been reduced to alphabetized lingerie drawers and imported French dairy substitutes? Where is the child in this home?"

"A perfect size 2, Mrs. X devotes herself to maintaining her good looks, the pristine elegance of her lavish apartment (there's a full-time housekeeper of course) and making sure Grayer does not muss up her PRADA togs."

"Both parents see their children as a prestige accessory, not as a little boy with enormous unmet emotional needs."

"Mr. X is too busy with his thong-sporting mistress."

So what does all this tell us?
1. You may get rich, but that doesn't mean you'll be happy.
2. Rich people don't raise their own kids.
3. Rich women are too busy socializing to actually spend time with their children.
4. Thin people are egotistical.
5. Rich women are vain, vapid and superficial.
6. Rich men are workaholics who don't care about their family, but, rather, only about making money.
7. Rich people are adulterers.

Now notice that neither the book author nor the reporter actually say any of these things. They simply present "evidence" to let you come to these conclusions.

Which leads us to the question, why would anyone *want* to believe all these things about thin, rich, or successful people?

Because it validates their life of quiet desperation.

If you are overweight and out of shape, it's good to know that those who are very thin aren't necessarily happy. Because, let's face it, that would really be too much. If we knew that they were thin *and* happy—that might be more than we can bear.

And, if we know that rich people are poor parents—we can feel noble for being broke. If we learn that wealthy people are vain, stupid, and cheat on their spouses—then we can justify why we never opened that business, went after that promotion, or acted on our dream.

Most people spend all day parroting useless information they were programmed from gossip and the various media outlets. As much as we love them, some of our best friends can unwittingly be our worst enemies just by being themselves. They'll talk about how bad the economy is, the latest train wreck they heard about on the news, someone's heart attack, or who's cheating on whom. You need to make sure that people do not sabotage your philosophy of abundance.

If you have ever heard me present my "Conquer Self-Doubt, Create Destiny" keynote speech, then you've heard me talk about the movie, "Titanic." This is probably the most evil movie ever made—programming you on level after level that money is bad, rich people are evil, and it is spiritual to be poor. So of course it became the most popular movie of all time.

Why?

Because it panders to your lack programming.

The big hit last year was "Spiderman." It was such a success, in big part, because it was filled with insidious lack and limitation messages. If this didn't jump out at you from the screen while you watched it, then you've got a ways to go in your consciousness in this area.

Here are just some of the subliminal messages this movie foists upon you:

Poverty is noble.   We have the poor relatives who bring up Peter, the poor orphan. (By the way, have you ever noticed how many orphans there are in popular literature? Not just Spiderman, but Batman is an orphan, Superman is, Harry Potter is, and plenty more are. This is to evoke emotional support from you.) There even is a part in the movie, where Peter's uncle speaks the most lack-centered words that have ever been spoken.

"We may be poor, but at least we are honest!"

Translation to your subconscious mind: Rich people are crooks.

Which is subliminal message number two. The evil villain in the movie, is, of course, the billionaire industrialist. He is wealth and ambition personified—the devil incarnate!

These messages were repeated over and over . . .

Remember the scene where Peter finally gets up the nerve to talk to the neighbor girl. She seems like she cares for him, then the rich kid shows up with his new car (that daddy bought him for his birthday). She drops Peter like a piece of radioactive camel dung and jumps in the new car and speeds off.

Is it any wonder that you grow up hating rich people and subconsciously not wanting to be like them? Once this is ingrained in you, the guilt starts. And it is that guilt that can stop you from accepting the abundance you are meant to have! Next, we'll look at how that plays out.

Chapter Four
The Virtue of Selfishness

So we know that you've been programmed by the "data-sphere" (TV, radio, newspaper, family, friends, email, etc.) since you were very young. Just how does that play out in causing you to hold back?

First you realize that you might embarrass your family. Then it dawns on you that your friends might not like you any more. Then, if you start to manifest prosperity, the lack-programmed people around you start with the comments.

"You paid how much for that! Isn't that a bit much?"

"How much do you need anyway?"

And, of course, my favorite, "Children are starving in Africa, and you paid $___ for ____!?"

You start to feel guilty when you buy nice things. If you have great health, or a wonderful relationship, you start to downplay them around friends that don't have them. You hide your light under a bushel, because you want to fit in. You may start degrading yourself with self-depreciating humor around them. And, pretty soon, you start to believe these comments yourself.

I am writing this section of the book, aboard British Airways Flight 001, also known as the Concorde.   Now this is what I call prosperity. When you can get on a plane in New York, and a few hours later you can be in London, in time for afternoon tea! I can't wait to go back on Monday. I get home an hour and a half before I left!

So when is something too much?

It costs about twelve grand to ride this baby. A nine or ten-hour ride on a regular jet is about $5,000 to sit up front. If you shop around, you can get the cattle car section for less than $800.

How much is your time worth? How much is your comfort worth? Would you feel guilty if you spent $12,000 on a plane ride? If so, why would you feel guilty? Have you ever sat down and analyzed where these guilt feelings come from? Would you agree that the programming we discussed has a lot to do with that?

Did any of the guilt you have or have had in the past come from the idea that if you are getting something good—it means someone else is getting something bad? That's what happens for a lot of people. It's all based upon a belief in lack and finite resources.

If you're like most people, you would feel very guilty spending $12,000 on the Concorde, feeling the extra money spent could feed the homeless, be given to the church, used to cure cancer, etc. The foundation of that is that there is only one $12,000. That you could spend it to fly, or do good work, but not both. It is based on the supposition that money is finite.

Nothing could be further from the truth . . .

Because you can spend $12,000 to fly the Concorde AND send $12,000 to the shelter, church, or charity. You just have to make more money! And if you don't know how—learn! (Which this series of books will greatly help you do.)

Money—like love, substance, and other resources—is INFINITE. All these resources can be infinitely replenished, simply by you manifesting more.

I once got a letter from someone who was in the audience at a church when I did the service. I had shared a story about flying First Class to Tahiti, and staying in a bungalow over the water, where I could feed the fish from a window in the floor. I explained how money was infinite, I could travel in style, and still do many good things.

She was less than impressed with my reasoning, wondering if I shared my infinite financial resources with the people "living in desperate poverty" a few miles down the road from my "lavish accommodations." She also wondered if I would "give some of those infinite resources to a single mother who is working two jobs and can't afford to go to Opa Locka, no less Tahiti."

The basis of comments like these is of course, "You have plenty, and others don't. They need it. You should feel very guilty for this, and start giving away all your money until you are back at the level of the poor people around you."

THIS IS THE KIND OF EVIL BELIEF THAT KEEPS SO MANY PEOPLE BROKE!

It is based on the idea that people who have wealth should disburse it to the unfortunate ones who don't. Why? Because they don't have it. They "need" it.

This is completely anti-prosperity and anti-humanity, because it completely disregards the laws of prosperity and human dignity. Prosperity and dignity are both based upon value given for value received (a/k/a you reap what you sow).

True prosperity is based upon the concept of selfishness. Yes, selfishness.

How does that make you feel when I tell you that? How do you feel when someone else calls you selfish?

What would you think if I told you that selfishness is good? In fact, selfishness is your moral prerogative.

Ayn Rand wrote a book entitled, "The Virtue of Selfishness." When asked why she chose to use a word that threatened so many people, she replied, "For the reason that makes you afraid of it."

I, like Rand did, use the word "selfish" to describe virtuous qualities of character. Let me explain . . .

The dictionary definition of selfishness is basically *concern with one's own interests, without regard for others.* It means, I value myself first, regardless of what anyone else thinks. Notice that there is no good or evil implicit in the definition. That, 'without regard for others,' does not mean that you are doing harm to others. It simply means that you are well adjusted and sensible enough to meet your own needs first. Now of course that's not what most of society, or 'the tribe,' would have you believe . . .

They tell you it is your moral imperative to put the interests of the many before the interests of the one. That you should sacrifice yourself for the "greater good."

This idea is very dangerous to your self-esteem and your life. Relinquishing your happiness for the sake of others, known or unknown, verifies to yourself, and others, that you are small and unworthy of even your own attention. It's actually anti-humanity, and it makes you mentally sick!

Your survival and your pursuit of happiness must form the foundation of your value system. To make your life, by your own means, towards your own standards, and for your own enjoyment. Anything less than that is harmful to you. And anything harmful to the individual is actually detrimental to society as a whole.

But don't think "society" is smart enough to figure that out. It's not.

The tribe will maintain that the needs of the individual should be relinquished to the needs of the masses. They will tell you that it is your responsibility to take care of the less fortunate.

Sounds innocent enough, doesn't it? Well let's take a look . . .

One Saturday you're out watering your lawn when a car drives up and you recognize your old friend Eddie at the wheel. You learn that he has just lost his job; his wife has kicked him out; and he couldn't think of anywhere else to go.

Eddie has always been in the middle of some drama or another, which is the main reason you haven't spoken too much lately. But you feel sorry for him and invite him in to crash for the night. The next day, Eddie asks if you wouldn't mind if he stays just a couple more nights until he can find an apartment, and he assures you that he has a job all lined up. You feel a little awkward, but agree anyway. During the week, the job falls through and although you feel badly about it, you haven't failed to notice that he isn't making much of an effort to go out and find another.

A week turns into two, and soon you don't feel like coming home from your office. You feel like your home is no longer your own. You resent the position you find yourself in, yet you feel guilty about being so selfish. After all, the guy has nowhere to go. Then you walk into your house and, once again, find Eddie sitting in your lounger, drinking beer, and watching your TV . . .

Freeze frame.

I could go on, but you get the picture.   What's the surface situation here?

The tribe mentality says that poor Eddie has caught a bad break, and since he's your friend, you owe it to him to help him out. You've been lucky; Eddie has fallen on misfortune.

There you sit in a beautiful big home, with a lovely landscaped yard, and he has nothing. Not only does he not have a job, but now his car is broken and he doesn't have money to fix it. He couldn't get a new car because the bank wouldn't approve his credit. "They only lend money to people who don't need it."

He's having a hard time getting a job because he needs to be paid cash, because creditors are hounding him and would garnish his wages. His "bitch" ex-wife is also harassing him for money.

Truth is, you have a little money saved. You have a car and a house. You work, and you'll get another paycheck this Friday. Eddie has not a penny. He "needs" it. You don't. And you probably feel guilty, because you have so much, and Eddie has so little.

This is exactly what moochers like Eddie count on to take advantage of you. But let's look a little deeper...

Five years ago, you and Eddie worked at the same place. He was out the door every day at five sharp. "We're on salary," he said. "You don't get paid extra to stay late." But you stayed late many times anyway, because you had projects to finish, and you wanted a clean desk in the morning. Eddie got a head start on "Happy Hour" at the bar. When there were extra projects to do, you volunteered for them. Eddie told you that you were stupid for doing so. When time for raises and promotions came, you got them.

Eddie quit after a year because they were "cheap, and they play favorites."

Each month, you set aside a little money for savings and your house fund. Eddie couldn't do that because he wasn't "making enough money." His priorities were nightlife at the clubs, cigarettes, getting a DVD player, cable TV, and the other "necessities" of life.

You went without cable to put the extra $30 a month into your retirement plan. Instead of first-run movies, you usually caught them for $3 when the videos came out. You didn't buy a DVD because you thought the money was better put into your savings account. You lived on less than what you made, and invested the balance in your future.

The tribe would tell you that, "Poor Eddie can't catch a break." In reality, all the strikes against him are self-created. <u>The situation he is in right now is the result of thousands of little choices he made every day</u>.

He spends six bucks a day on cigarettes because, "the damn tobacco companies got me addicted." He buys a 12-pack of beer twice a week because he "needs to relax." The reason his ex-wife is after him is because he hasn't paid child support payments in two years. The reason the bank wouldn't finance a new car was because he has a legal judgment against him for the student loans he took out and never paid back, after he dropped out of college.

He has always spent more than he earned, and now, when he is facing a setback, he has no resources to fall back on. So he develops a "victim" mentality. This victim-hood role he is in causes others to feel guilty, and, thus, they are constantly bailing him out from one thing or another. He learns how to manipulate his tragedies for maximum effect.

Of course, all the time he is "owning" this victim-hood, he is programming his subconscious mind to attract more drama, more tragedy, and more challenges. He has learned that he can ignore the laws of prosperity and live for the moment, because there is always someone to save him from paying the price. So he goes on an endless victim cycle, always in one situation or another. He's forever getting laid off, left out, and wronged.

So what's the good thing to do? What's the "Christian" thing to do? The "right" thing? Should you help him?

Well, I think the answer is "maybe." But before we address that, let's look at what is going to happen anyway . . .

Today's social system is ready to catch Eddie in its safety net. The government will feed, clothe and house Eddie. They have dozens and dozens of social programs for countless contingencies, and they can fund all of them because they force you to contribute from your paycheck each week. If you refuse, they will put you in prison.

What if, instead of paying your taxes to the government on payday, things went like this. You receive your paycheck, and, depending on where you live in the world, you immediately cut a check for 35%, 58% or 62% of your wages, which would normally represent your income taxes, and you hop into your average sedan and head on over to Eddie's.

Eddie is on his porch sipping from a can of beer and eyes you malevolently as you pull up. Hopping enthusiastically out of your car, you approach him, check in hand.

"Hey Eddie!" you say. "Just thought I'd pop by with your check seeing as how I was on my way home. There you go. Another month of food, clothing, medical care, dental, entertainment. And because of the raise I received last week, there's a little more in there for your pension. Well, I can see you're into things. Is there, uh, anything else I can do for you? No? Well, I'll be off then. Have a ton of paperwork to clear up tonight! Have a wonderful evening, Eddie! Take it easy. See you next month!"

Would you ever agree to such a thing? In reality, you already have, because that's the end result of the government taxation system today. It is currently set up in a manner that the productive are penalized and the unproductive are rewarded. Where receiving something unearned is a sought-after commodity.

The result of this dysfunctional system is that it disintegrates your self-esteem. Constantly sacrificing yourself, your values, for others in order to either gain a sense of moral superiority, or in order to escape some sense of anxiety or guilt, continually weakens your resolve. Without resolve, your confidence is at stake. You question your own worth and feel guilty when you do things to take care of yourself.

A strong resolve and a complete refusal to live by any other standard than that which holds with your values is the key to healthy, abundant self-esteem. It is only by being strong yourself that you can help others. Those whom you love and value, and whom you admire because their values are akin to your own.

The next time you taxi for takeoff aboard an airplane, notice that during the safety presentation, you are advised to put on your own oxygen mask before helping another don theirs. Help people out of strength, if you choose to do so, not out of weakness.

I am convinced that a lack of selfishness is self-destructive. Adopting self-sacrifice as a virtue enables others to take complete advantage of you and, practiced long enough, selfless behavior destroys.

I just got off the phone with a friend of mine who is a general manger at a restaurant. He had just fired a waiter who was his friend and who had worked there for nine years. The waiter was supposed to be at work at six on Sunday morning. He called at 5:50 to say he was sick. He was supposed to report Monday at seven. He never showed up, or even called. He showed up at a staff meeting on Tuesday and was disrespectful and disruptive. It became apparent that he had gone back to using drugs again. So my friend fired him.

Sound cold and uncaring?

Nothing could be further from the truth. In fact, my friend was sick over having to fire this guy. But it is this kind of "tough love" that has the best chance of getting this individual to accept responsibility for his actions and turn his life around.

Take a businessman who keeps a terrible employee because he feels sorry for her. He hasn't the heart to fire her because her life is a wreck; her mother is an alcoholic; her father ran out; her husband's in jail—whatever—and so he enables her self-destructive behavior and lifestyle by keeping her on.

In keeping this employee, against his better judgment, but for the moral good—his other employees must take up her slack. They begin to feel resentful and angry. Performance suffers across the board. Even hardworking, dedicated employees start to slack, because they see that they are not treated and rewarded in respect to the effort they contribute. Your customers receive poor service and soon your business is in real trouble.

But lets say, the businessman had done things differently, selfishly, for the betterment of himself and his company. He calls the errant worker into his office and after explaining why, fires her. Perhaps this turns out to be the wake-up call she needed and, giving her head a shake, and she sets out to improve her attitude and get a better job. One that she can be selfishly happy in. And if not, at the least he has a company that isn't in jeopardy and a happy crew to work with.

Equally destructive is the wife who covers for the abuses of her husband. Year after year, she puts up with a steady torrent of emotional and physical terror. She looks 50 on her 30th birthday, and is so frail a strong northerly wind would knock her down.   A love story gone horribly wrong.

Imagine though, if she had been strong in her resolve, had confidence in her own values, and had walked away after the first abuse. She would have selfishly saved herself from a life of despair rather than live as a sacrificial animal at the hand of a brute.

In a free society, where the needs of the individual come first, people are liberated from guilt and anxiety. <u>Self-sacrifice is more than the root of low self-esteem. It is anti-prosperity, and consequently anti-humanity</u>. Because when the living energy of productive citizens is sucked from them by the parasitic tribe—what incentive is there to remain productive?

<u>Every man and woman of integrity should earn their own living in the fair and free trade of value for value with others</u>. This means no free rides. No pride in receiving the unearned.

Let me share a hypothetical situation I created after being inspired by something my friend Stuart Goldsmith wrote in his newsletter.

Imagine, for this moment that we are flying to Bali for a Mastermind Council Retreat, and the plane goes down. We are stranded on a deserted island together with 20 other families. Being so isolated and completely exposed to the elements, we all quickly go about the construction of shelters and huts from the abundance of bamboo around the island. We search out a fresh water source, which we find located halfway up the back side of a mountain, a 2-hour hike from the camp.

Fortunately there are crab and fish, clams and mussels in the surrounding sea as well as palm and fruit trees, so with a little ingenuity and skill, food abounds. All in all, between hunting and gathering, reinforcing our huts, building fires and cooking food . . . after looking after the survival needs of our families every day, we all fall into our makeshift palm-frond beds at night exhausted.

Being a small group, we soon find that by working with others and exchanging values, we can get the work done a bit more efficiently. So we all start making deals. I'll go get the water and firewood for my family and yours today if you will spend the day fixing up the roof of my hut. And tomorrow, while I spend the day digging clams and collecting coconuts for our two families, you spend the day getting the firewood and the water.

Great . . . we're getting things done, but we're not making much forward progress.

Progress is to our greatest advantage because it is always done in the spirit of making things easier. For freeing up time away from the toil and drudgery in order to get more out of life. More time, more freedom, more enjoyment.

So, one day, while lying on your back feeling completely battered after sliding 100 feet back down the incline leading to the water source, you come up with a brilliant idea. What if you could rig up a pipe system with bamboo shafts, thereby bringing the water to the camp and saving yourself the agony of hauling water?

Fantastic! But how on earth are you going to have the time for such a huge project while you have to worry about the long, daily grind of feeding and sheltering your family?

You work extra. While everyone else is resting at night, you labor an extra two hours each day, building your pipeline. After weeks of strenuous effort, you're done.

That evening around the campfire, you stand up and make the following proposal:

"Every day you spend your morning trudging up the mountain to bring back water. I have designed and built a pipeline that brings the water direct to the village. I am willing to trade it for fish, coconuts, clothing, and other products of your labor. In a fair exchange of value, we can trade.

"You win, because you don't have to climb the mountain for four hours every day. I win, because I don't have to spend so much time fishing, hunting and farming. All you have to do on every hot tropical day, is walk out of your hut to the middle of our community and pour yourself an icy cold drink of mountain bubbly."

In exchange for the use of your pipeline, each family agrees to trade one hour of labor, hunting, or gathering for your family. That means that your innovative piping system will save them three, of their previous four hours of collecting water each day. You of course save 19 hours, because of all the things you get in trade. You have been rewarded for your ingenuity and innovation.

Your motivation was selfish, yet you benefited everyone in the community.

You were creative, and put out the effort. It wasn't easy for you to haul bamboo all over the mountain, to fit it or bind it, but YOU did it. And you deserve to feel pride. You have just created nineteen hours of labor-saving for yourself. You used to work 12 hours a day. Now you have the benefit of 19. Which means you have a surplus of seven hours worth of supplies.

So you decide to open up a *7-8* store, which is open each evening from seven to eight. You barter the excess goods you have for other things. You continue to trade and collect more things. Pretty soon, you're putting on a new addition to your hut. You add a billiard room and build a deck out back. Next thing you know, you've added a three-bike garage and built a pool in the back yard. You are reaping the reward of your labor and innovation.

Notice that no one was forced into this agreement. If they don't want to trade an hour labor with you, they can continue to climb the mountain and fetch their own water each day. Of course no one does, because that would be stupid, causing him or her an extra three hours work.

Now your neighbor Fred is inspired by your invention. He decides to use the three hours that he used to spend in collecting water, building a sturdy boat from a hollowed-out tree. He can now go out to the deeper water, where the big fish are. He fashions a net from weaving palm fronds and snares many large fish at a time, instead of waiting for the few to come in around the rocks and trying to spear them.

He opens *Fred's Fish House,* with an all-you-can-eat fish fry every Friday night. The fish is delicious, and the fish fry turns into "the place to be" every week. It gets so busy that your neighbor hires the lady from hut six to help him serve everybody. He hires the guy from hut 11 to mix pineapple and mango coolers. This part-time work earns them some extra coconuts, which they can trade with others to get goods and services they need.

Meanwhile Fred is doing great. He opens a second location, on the other side of the island. Since he's the founder of the island's first successful restaurant chain, he becomes a motivational speaker. His inspirational, you-can-do-this-too, "rags to rattan" story inspires millions of people (ok, pairs of people) all over the world (ok, the island).

He can now lounge around making gimp bracelets all day. You and Fred design a golf course to occupy your afternoons. He takes up playing conga drums made of coconuts, and you squeeze out some different colored berries and start to paint landscapes. It is the beginning of the arts on your little island.

Possibilities in paradise surround you. *Of course, the other families, who have yet to make timesaving innovations of their own, see things a little differently . .*

In fact, they seem to have completely forgotten that the two of you have saved them hours of time and work with your inventions. They see you lounging in your hammock, while they're out grubbing for berries. They start to get jealous and resentful, because it's "not fair."

They call a town meeting, and decide to elect a government. Someone runs on a "populist for the people" platform and they're elected in a landslide, 18 to 2.   They immediately introduce a socialist system, "for the good of the many."   They need to pay themselves, hire inspectors for the water pipeline, and people to license the fishing boat, sweep the dirt floor at the new city hall, etc., so they start an income tax system.

Village members start to grumble. This doesn't look so good. They don't like the idea of paying taxes.

Then the new mayor announces that everyone has a "right" to water and big fish, so he's going to nationalize the pipeline and fishing industry. The government takes away your pipeline and Fred's boat is stolen from him as well. Now the villagers are nodding along. They realize that they no longer have to trade an hour of labor a day to you and Fred. The government is going to provide for them. They don't mind paying their taxes, because they realize that this allows them to tax their way into the wallets of you and Fred. Now things are getting "fair." Your little island has just started on the path to Socialism, which is simply Communism with lipstick.

This is now the beginning of the end . . .

In this scenario, the uninspired islanders would, out of resentment, 'seize the means of production' in the name of the public. If you resisted, you would be imprisoned or executed as an 'enemy of the state.' The tribe would be happy, because now they have free access to the water and fishing boat. (Of course it's not free, but they get more back from their taxes than they pay in, so they couldn't care less.)

But what would happen next?

Kathy, who had an idea how to harness wind and solar power for electricity would figure, why bother? Fernando, who had an idea for a coconut husker would think the same thing. They would rightly conclude that the extra labor and resources they devote to innovation would never be rewarded, because the government would steal the excess they created, and distribute it to the moochers.

Progress and innovation would stop. Cures for diseases would never be found; inventions would not be created; and life would continue to be a primitive struggle for survival. In fact, they would only continue to look for free handouts, and eventually, the little collective would shrivel up and die.

The world has seen that Communism does not work. All over the globe, it has failed miserably. The last real remnant is Cuba, a nation that is completely bankrupt. The experiment in Socialism has failed just as desperately. What we call free enterprise in the western world is actually just a watered-down version of Socialism. A system not unlike our fictional island government.

Now, why am I telling you all this?

It's not to discuss the politics, as fascinating as that may be. It's to help you realize the lack and limitation programming you have been assaulted with since you were young. And make you understand that <u>the very system you live in is creating subconscious programming that makes you feel guilty for succeeding, and rewards you for doing less than you are capable of</u>. It creates codependent dysfunctional people. <u>If you accept this thinking, your chances for real success are almost non-existent</u>.

As creative-thinking human beings, we are up against a mass of people who want something for nothing and governments around the world who want to give it to them.

The sad truth is that your government doesn't want you to be successful. Your government wants and needs you to be a worker drone in the collective to support their system of giving money away to keep themselves reelected.

Governments don't want you to be too successful for other reasons as well...

If you are super-productive and your idea hits mainstream, you may earn billions of dollars like Bill Gates and other billionaires. This makes you an alarming threat. With that kind of money you could topple a government.

If you're freethinking, you might choose to opt out of the system and go your own way. How, then, would the government make a profit from your life's effort? Without the means to tax its citizens, how would the government stay in power? After all, it is their distorted Robin Hood platform that has gotten them elected by the mooching masses.

The plain truth is that a productive, innovative, intelligent human being in today's world has to be strong in his or her resolve in order to rise above the looters and parasites, to live a rewarding and prosperous life.

On your journey to self-fulfillment, you will find that it is not just your government that doesn't want you to be successful; it is also sometimes your community, your friends, and your family.

Let's take this example of a true story. In a small city there lives a local media mogul. Over his career, he has used his considerable business acumen to acquire various newspapers, after which he would run and sell them for a profit. He builds a gargantuan mansion on beautiful oceanfront property, large enough to support his wife's hobby. She grows flowers and sells them on the local market.

Being a savvy businessman, he looks into the tax situation and finds a way to save on his property taxes. His wife's flower business qualifies as hobby farm status, and, registered as such, would reduce their property tax to one-tenth of what he was paying. For more than a few years, she sells her flowers in the community and is recognized locally for her love of gardening. So, he goes ahead with the registration.

A local reporter, who probably isn't making more than $25,000 to 30,000 a year, gets wind that Mr. Mogul and his entrepreneur wife are making the most of a tax write-off. Being of socialist bent, he writes a scathing article in the local newspaper. How dare such a wealthy man, who owns so much, and has so much, be so criminal as to cheat the system on his taxes?

Soon, the community is in an uproar. How dare they! The cottage on the property is bigger than most people's homes! Look at the cars they drive! The socialist outcry... "What about the non-productive people? Don't they get a break? Why should the moguls be able to save on their property taxes when so many people can't?"

Well, for one thing, most people don't turn their hobby into a thriving part-time business! The outcry was loud enough that local government officials were pressured to change the laws. They stripped away the hobby farm status, and across the city, a collective sigh of relief was heard.

Why is it that normally apathetic people get irate at the thought of anyone who prospers from their own ingenuity? I believe it is because they are so deeply ingrained in poverty-consciousness that they resent people who are wealthy. They become envious of people who are succeeding.

I certainly experienced this growing up. I remember being so jealous of other kids who went on vacations, who had mini-bikes, go-carts, and other toys my family couldn't afford. When I got to be driving age, I looked at the kids who could afford to get cars right away, and I got even more jealous.

I saw people living in nicer houses, and I always wondered why it was that they should get all that stuff, and not me. I believe a lot of people do that.   Once you adopt this tribe thinking, you become a victim. Just like our friend Eddie that we began this chapter with.

What happened in my case was—unbeknownst to me— on a subconscious level, I began to hate rich people and think they were bad. Thing was, I very much wanted to be rich myself. (Or, at least, that's what I believed.) In fact, I wanted to be a millionaire by the time I was 35. I spent just about every waking moment thinking about wealth. I wanted more out of life; I didn't like being broke.

The problem was, <u>I still had the underlying belief that rich people were bad</u>.

So even though I said I wanted to be wealthy, I was doing things on a daily basis that were taking me further away from wealth. From my work, to the people I hung out with, from dysfunctional relationships, to a complete lack of self-development—I was thinking like the people around me.

And we all thought like victims.

And this is how the majority of people walk around every day. They are completely in conflict with themselves. Victims of their own subconscious programming.

Fortunately, I hit bottom. And when I had absolutely nothing, I was able to let all the negative thinking go, as well. With my blank slate, I started to fill my life with knowledge, ideas, and pursuits that would bring me into harmony with the prosperity I sought.

I didn't do it by keeping the same people around me and staying in the same pattern of thinking, however . . .

When you start adopting beliefs of abundance and prosperity, you stop putting things into your body that make you sick; you stop taking actions that get you into trouble; and you stop hanging out with dysfunctional people, because they bring you down. None of it appeals to you anymore.

Instead, you start eating right and feeling great! With that energy and vitality, you take actions that bring you prosperity. When you honor your values, you start to meet people who celebrate the same things in life that you do.

In our present, mass-driven world, there are billions of people who think from lack. I'd say most of the world's religions preach lack, the education systems teach lack, and that we are part of a human race that believes that rewards come to those who are good, but poor.

Whether you believe it or not, the masses have chosen poverty, regardless of the fact that they wish they had money. The media, television networks and advertisers work to reflect those beliefs that appeal to the masses' need of acceptance. Our culture celebrates mediocrity.

It takes a very brave person to follow their dreams. We are often ridiculed for having higher ideas and goals. It is most unfortunate that this kind of discouragement often begins in our homes with family and friends.

If you think this to be untrue, I'd like you to close your eyes in a moment and imagine that it is New Year's Day and your home is filled with your family and friends. In a moment of inspiration, you silence everyone and announce that it is your intent, for this New Year, to become a billionaire!

In the overwhelming silence or amusement that follows, how will you feel? Do you immediately recant and say you were just kidding to let everyone off the hook? How do you feel now just thinking about it?

In school, I'm sure you were never taught about prosperity. Now, I have good friends who are teachers, and I do believe that many teachers do make a difference. Most, however, teach their students to be "realistic" with their hopes and dreams. They may encourage someone who wants to be an Internet multi-millionaire to "get realistic" and settle for a $30,000 job in the corporate environment.

While thinking they are doing their students a favor by telling them how it is out there in the real world, from their reality, they are doing them a disservice by quashing their aspirations.

Family works the same way. Not to say that they don't mean well. I'm sure that, in their own way, most of them do. Parents teach their kids to go for the secure jobs, and maybe even get Union wages if they're lucky! Grandparents talk about how good the kids have it now compared to when they grew up. They reminisce about the Depression and how much worse it was then.

Home is where we learn to watch television. And you know how I feel about TV and the programming you get there. By the way, have you ever seen a commercial for a $100,000 necklace? For your own private jet? Rolls Royce?

Actually you don't see too many advertisements for anything remotely prosperous. Mainly it's the latest $1.99 meal at McDonald's, or for a plastic plaything for the kids. Beer and cola commercials abound. Come, shop at Wal-Mart!

The irony is that the masses have their reality reflected back at them and it's all lack-conscious low-end stuff. This lack-consciousness is what the masses buy into. It's what they wear; what they see; what they eat. I have friends and family that are a part of that massreality. Who have bought it all and live it day to day.

As I said before, you have to be brave to make a break from this type of thinking, or non-thinking. A lot of people find this a huge stumbling block. There is a lot of fear tied up in leaving the pack.

If we're successful, won't our friends and family think we're bad people? They think other rich people are bad – why not us? If I tell my friends my hopes and dreams, will they ridicule me? Will they snicker and say stuff behind my back? If I quit my 'secure' job to do what I've always dreamed of, will he or she leave me? What if I try really hard and fail? Will everyone laugh? If my house is bigger than my parents', will they harbor resentment? Will they stop loving me?

Fear of success is a direct result of low self-esteem and a lack of selfishness. You'll notice all those questions are about other people and not about the one person whose happiness is really on the line. You.

Think prosperity! Recognize lack consciousness and banish it from your thoughts. Catch yourself in the role of the self-sacrificing martyr and regain your self-respect. Every person on this planet deserves to experience abundance. Every person on this planet is capable of great things.

One of our greatest scientists is a quadriplegic. Some of our finest athletes can be found at the Special Olympics. Every person is capable of great things if they only put their mind to it.

But to do this, you must be capable of critical thought. Which is something the herd cannot yet do.

Put another way—they don't know how to think. They have been told WHAT to think for so long, they no longer know HOW to think. What's the lesson for you?

Most people are stupid. Sheep-led-to-the-slaughter stupid. Mindless automatons following their programming. And I'm not trying to sound mean or unsympathetic. But if you want true prosperity, I have to tell you the truth.

If you want to accept your abundance—you need to be a contrarian.

The reason most people are living lives of quiet desperation, is that they are incapable of discernment. The reason Bill Gates is a billionaire, is because he can discern things that others can't.

He questions things. He wonders, "What if?" "Why?" and "Why not?" He is to discern the difference between something that is because it makes sense—and something that is because "everybody does it that way." Bill Gates is a contrarian.

So were Henry Ford, J. Paul Getty, Andrew Carnegie, Leonardo di Vinci, Marconi, Edison, Einstein, and all the brilliant thinkers throughout history. Successful people don't think like the pack. They question everything.

Since we're talking about Bill Gates, let's compare the way he thinks, with the way most people think. I was waiting in an airport lounge, when I picked up a copy of a major business magazine. It had a column by Stuart Alsop, criticizing Microsoft and Gates. Headlined, "The right thing to regulate," he perpetuates the assertion that Microsoft is a monopoly, and speaks out for the government action against it.

What an easy target. One that is sure to be popular with the tribe. Why, everybody can agree that Microsoft is the "death star," destroying everything in its way until it controls the world. I mean, Gates is worth what—$40, $50, $60 billion? How much is enough, for crying out loud, right?

Wrong. Very, very wrong.

When a simple-minded writer like Alsop panders to the lack and limitation beliefs of his readers—he simply demonstrates his lack of understanding of how capitalism and free enterprise work.

When someone asked Ayn Rand why Americans are so anti-intellectual, she replied that it was because America's intellectuals are so anti-American.

I find it simply amazing that a magazine that is supposed to be an icon of free enterprise could print such silly socialist nonsense. But, of course, they do.

What do you think happens to you, when you read such inane drivel? It programs you for lack. You see yourself as a helpless victim of the billion-dollar corporation, needing the government to "save" you from its abuses.

What is Microsoft's crime? That they created software that millions of people want to use. Millions of people like me—who are not that computer savvy—have learned that we can actually work a computer that uses the Windows operating system.

But wait, you say. Didn't the U.S. government say that Microsoft was bundling their Internet browser with the operating system, therefore strangling trade, and creating a monopoly?

(Sigh.) Here's the analogy. Suppose Tony Robbins and I are doing a seminar on the same weekend, we're both in Chicago. I offer a free tape album with your seminar registration. Should Tony sue? Petition the government? He could claim unfair trade, restraint of trade, and monopoly.

Or, why doesn't he just offer a free tape album with his own seminar? Or, better yet, he could offer two!

You see the government does not need to legislate seminar companies, control prices, and determine value. If you let free enterprise work—it will take care of the consumer all by itself. Competition is what keeps prices low and values high.

If you are serious about manifesting prosperity in your life—Bill Gates should be one of the heroes at the top of your list. And Microsoft should be treated by the U.S. government like what it really is—a true American success story.

It's easy to depict Microsoft as the billion-dollar monster, devouring everything in its path. That's what Alsop and the majority of the mainstream media do. It's easy pickings—pandering to Joe Lunchbucket.

These deceptions ignore one very simple fact. Microsoft is a company formed by a couple of kids who dropped out of college—because they had an idea and a dream. Gates and Paul Allen created a company based on innovation and attracted people like Richard Brody, and legions of other bright people.

The thing that will ultimately control Microsoft is not government regulation. It is the fact that right now, all over the world, there are other bright kids sitting in a dorm room somewhere with nothing but empty pizza boxes—who will come up with the next development in software—one that could make Word, Excel, Explorer or even Windows obsolete.

And they will do this, driven by the desire to live the American dream, as personified by Gates, Allen, and the thousands of other millionaires created by Microsoft.

Yet if you read the business and computer trade magazines—you'll slowly get programmed to believe that Microsoft is bad, and Gates is the enemy. That's why you have to have discernment. Question what you read and hear. Analyze why the tribe thinks the way it does. And think differently!

I used to live with a Colombian girl named Aura Alicia. One day we were lying on the sofa together, and she asked me to hand her purse to her. I did. She took out something, and I placed the purse on the floor next to me.

"No, no, no!" she exclaimed.

"What, what, what?" I replied, as I jerked the purse back up.

"The floor is no place for a purse," she replied.

"Oh, I'm sorry," I responded, as I put the purse back on the chair.

About 30 seconds later, I started laughing. Aura wanted to know what was so funny. The more she asked, the harder I laughed. Finally I composed myself enough to explain.

I told her that "The floor is no place for a purse" just didn't seem right coming from her. It sounded like something her grandmother would have said. (We were probably both about 28 at that time.) And just exactly why was the floor no place for a purse, I wanted to know.

She thought about it for a few seconds and began to laugh herself. She had no idea why the floor was no place for a purse. She just remembered once as a little girl putting her mother's purse on the floor and receiving that admonishment. It lodged into her subconscious programming, and came into view more than 20 years later.

We start to learn things by the time we're two years old—and most people never question them. Prosperous people do. And, by doing so, they gain new knowledge and fresh insights that others don't possess.

Not that long ago, cell phones were impossible. When Marconi suggested the radio, people knew he was insane. And Edison? Everyone knew what a crazy idea the light bulb was.

Yet, "everyone" is often wrong.

I'm convinced that the highest levels of success in sports, in business, and in life—come not so much from skill, training and ability—as they do from the mindset of the holder.

And this often requires you to think contrary to what the tribe is thinking. And ALWAYS requires you to question the beliefs you hold. On everything.

Do you know that if you move a goldfish to a lake – he will continue to swim in the same circle? Why? Because he has accepted the belief that if he swims farther, he's going to bump his nose. He's always done it this way. Any other way is "impossible."

When you question your beliefs—you question your limitations. If your beliefs serve you—they can withstand the scrutiny. If they don't survive the questioning—you can drop them, and replace them with beliefs that serve you.

Examples: You may have a belief that it's hard to succeed without a college education. That you need money to make money. That doing business in your big city/small town is hard. That people of your race have a harder time making it.

You may discover that these beliefs do not serve you, and decide to replace them with beliefs that do.

Examples:

Bill Gates and Paul Allen made it without a college education, I can too.

You need only a great idea to make money.

People in my city/town have already been successful, thus, I can be too.

Many people of my race are successful; no one can keep me down but myself.

By questioning the status quo, you prevent yourself from falling into a victim mentality, and developing fear, self-doubt, and lack. You recognize selfishness as a virtue and not an evil as the masses believe it to be. You realize that the government playing Robin Hood actually hurts everyone. Now this begs the question that may be troubling you . . .

Namely, what about the less fortunate? Should we just forget about them? Survival of the fittest?

No. We treat them with love, support, and compassion. But we do it ourselves, not at the point of a gun from the government.

The number one expense on my tax return each year is for charity. And it will be every year. I support causes for runaway kids, children with terminal diseases, animal protection organizations, my church, human rights, the Opera, the film festival, and a host of other causes. And you know what?

I can do that because I've been successful. When I was broke, I wasn't helping anyone. I enjoy supporting those causes, and I do it because I'm selfish. I give to them because of the joy it gives me to do so.

It sounds ironic, but it is quite true. If you want to help others, make a difference and leave behind some kind of legacy—it all begins with selfishness! Now, in the next chapter, we'll look at how that works with reason and purpose.

Chapter Five
The Purpose that Drives Your Life

"That's the difference with you," Dr. Peter Pearson remarked at dinner one night. (Peter is a member of my Mastermind Council.) "You really don't care what people think about you."

"That's true," I responded.

"No, I mean you *really* don't care!" he exclaimed.

Guilty as charged. Now I would be lying if I told you it was always that way. In fact, quite the opposite.

I could regale you with stories from my childhood and analyze where my insecurities came from – but what's the point? Existence exists. Things are what they are. Or as I have been known to tell guys in my seminars, "If I find your inner child, I'm going to kick his little ass!"

Yes, it's a fascinating story about when your mother tried to bronze your baby shoes while you were still in them. Likewise for the tale about how your father taught you to swim by rowing you out to the middle of the lake and throwing you overboard. And that by the time you cut your way out of the sack, he was gone.

At some point, you just have to let it go. Move on with your life. You have to be willing to give up your victim mentality and go past that, for that is where the real breakthroughs are.

Once you have strong self-esteem, you really don't care what others think of you. You really get that the responsibility is theirs, and has nothing to do with you. And this is a very important component of being able to accept your abundance.

So we've really got two issues here, both springing off of the same base. First is the issue of self-confidence, and the second is having a thought process different from most people. Not participating in "tribal thought."

In the last chapter, we looked at thinking differently for success. Now, I would like to take a closer look at how you develop the natural tendency to do just that.

It all begins with your fundamental core values. The things that are the most important to you, as this drives the actions you take every day. And these spring forth from your central purpose in life. Which immediately tells you why most people go through their entire lives sick, broke and stupid.

Now, I don't say that to be mean or arrogant, but we need to speak truth here. And the truth is that most people struggle through life simply reacting to events around them, oblivious to the fact that they help to create those events. Like a ship tossed at sea, they see themselves buffeted by external circumstances—a tiny object, subject to the wrath of the universe.

Most people are nowhere near ideal health. In fact, you could conservatively estimate that 80% of people suffer from obesity, low energy, poor cardiovascular capacity, disease, or a combination of those.

Most people are nowhere near wealthy. Now that may sound crass, in light of how much prosperity there appears to be in developed countries like the United States, Europe, Asia, and many other places. And there is no doubt that a great deal of progress has been made.

Even most people considered poor in those areas have good shelter, electricity, telephone, heating/air conditioning, and of course – TV. So they are wildly rich by the standards of the third world.

But here is the reality . . .

Most of these people have lots of "things" —but they are one hospital bill, or a two-week layoff from bankruptcy. Personal debt has never been higher, and personal savings have never been lower. These people give the appearance of being prosperous, but the reality is that they are broke.

Which brings us to door number three. Stupid. Just the fact that most people live their lives sick and broke tells us that they are not rocket scientists. And before you accuse me of arrogance and insensitivity, wait. I'm not happy that those people live that way, and I take no pleasure from it. And that is why I write this now, and do the work that I do. I am writing this book to help change that.

While I agree that many were born as victims of circumstances, I don't believe they have to stay that way . . .

I, myself, was born sick, broke and stupid, and lived almost 30 years in that condition. But I ultimately prevailed in rising above that, and I believe everyone can. I want you, and millions more like you, to taste the life of health, abundance, and intellectual stimulation. To look forward to each and every day with eager anticipation, passion and joy.

Now doing that, however, may require having a dramatic shift in your mindset, beliefs and opinion on life . . .

It may mean developing a life purpose for the first time, or replacing the one you have right now. And that may mean you have to dramatically alter the view you have of yourself, and your role in the world. If you're like most sick, broke and stupid people, you define yourself by your roles (husband, engineer, symphony board member, etc.), and you view your purpose through the eyes of servicing others, contributing to the greater good, or looking after the people around you.

If this is the case—you are insane. And you're no doubt sick, broke, and stupid!

Now if you haven't thrown this book away after that last statement, let me explain my comments. If you define yourself by your roles (Ray's wife, Becky's husband), then you have no personal identity. Which means you have a low self-esteem and opinion of yourself.

And if you see your main purpose in life as serving others, then you're probably personally responsible for the founding of at least three "Co-dependents Anonymous" chapters.

Let me go on the record and say, if your main purpose in life is to "serve others" —you have an extremely low opinion of yourself; don't believe you are worthy; and will experience a tremendous amount of lack and limitation in your life.

Now, you might come back with something like, "Really, I don't need all those outside things to be happy. I don't care about money and material things. A car just gets you from point A to point B. I am happy to live in a hut in the rain forest and teach the savages about Christianity. If I get enough grubs to eat and a thatched roof over my head, I am happy. I am serving others, which is the noble thing. I am doing God's work, and I will be rewarded in the afterlife."

Now, if you feel this way, please put this down right now, and back away from the book. Sell all of your possessions immediately, and join a cult.

You have a condition. A condition clinically termed insanity.

So why do I say that? Well, let's look at what exactly insanity is. I would define it as, "Unsoundness of mind to render a person unfit to maintain a relationship, or look after his or her own needs for emotional well-being and survival."

People who spend their existence worrying solely about the needs of others and not their own are not noble, benevolent, or spiritual. They are crazy.

<u>And, because they don't look after their own needs, they really can't help others in a healthy way</u>. They can console them, participate in their drama, or enable their co-dependence, but they can't offer them real, meaningful help. To repeat an oft-quoted line from a character from Ayn Rand's book, "The Fountainhead . . ."

"To say 'I love you,' one must first know how to say the word 'I.'"

You know that to love anyone else, you must first love yourself. But are you really aware of what that means on a practical application level? Rand taught, and I believe she was correct, that you must live your life by the fundamental values of:

Purpose.

Reason.

Self-esteem.

We've discussed the virtue of selfishness already. Now, let me really blow your mind. What do you think when I tell you that . . .

Your highest moral purpose must be your own happiness.

Does that threaten you? Offend you? Make you angry? If so, please take a good look at that. Because this is the only healthy, sane way to live. And the only way that ensures the survival of the species, and the well-being of the most people. In fact, it is the only honorable way to conduct any relationship!

You must not sacrifice yourself to others, because that is depravity. It is depravity because it is a certain state of moral corruption and degradation. It is sick—a sure symptom of mental illness.

Do you really get that?

And likewise for the opposite situation. You shouldn't ask others to sacrifice for you, for that is no less sick and depraved. Corrupting the morals of others is no less evil than corrupting your own.

Purpose . . .

It doesn't serve anyone to degrade yourself or to degrade others. And that is exactly what sacrificing yourself for others is.

In the book, "Atlas Shrugged," one of Ayn Rand's main characters is asked, "What is the most depraved kind of human being?" His answer would likely surprise most people, since he doesn't suggest a murderer, or rapist, or other sex offender. His answer is, "The man without a purpose."

When asked about why she suggested this as opposed to the other possibilities, Rand replied, "Because that aspect of their character lies at the root of and causes all the evils which you mentioned in your question. Sadism, dictatorship, or any form of evil, is the consequence of a man's evasion of reality. A consequence of his failure to think. The man without a purpose is a man who drifts at the mercy of random feelings or unidentified urges, and is capable of any evil, because he is totally out of control of his own life. In order to have control of your life, you have to have a purpose—a productive purpose."

When you have your own happiness as your highest moral purpose, you have a productive—and moral—reason to exist. Not only do you have a reason to exist, but also you exist in a state of true abundance!

And here's the important thing . . .

If everyone did this, the world would be a much better place! Instead of dysfunction, depravity, and codependence, we would have healthy, functional, value-for-value relationships. No one would be asking you to sacrifice for him or her, and you would behave the same way. That is the way healthy relationships are maintained.

Reason . . .

The next important fundamental value is running your life by reason. Which means that you analyze things with the criteria of whether it serves your highest moral purpose, which is the perpetuation of your happiness.

The question people ask me the most is, 'How do I know whether a belief I have is lack-oriented?' This is actually quite easy. Don't make it complicated. The question to ask is simply,

"Does this belief serve me?"

And the way to discern that is with your rational mind. Emotions are good. They are a vital part of living a full and rich life. But the truly sane and emotionally-balanced person will know—or will make it a point to discover— what is causing those emotions. There does not have to be a clash between your emotions and reason. And shouldn't be.

In "Breakthrough U," my Internet-based coaching program, I asked, "When I question a core belief of yours, are you furious with me because I'm 'wrong,' or because you are afraid to even ask the question?"

"When someone tells you that they love you and you are afraid—is it because you don't love them, or because you do, and you're afraid you'll lose them?"

"Is it really fear of failure that holds you back? Or is it really fear of success?"

So yes, you experience emotions. But don't make life-altering decisions based solely upon them. Feel your emotions, and then learn what causes them. Then, use your rational mind to decide what is in your highest good.

That means extend the situation to its logical conclusion, and see if the logic holds up. Meaning, check to ensure that if you pursue a particular course of action to its completion, it will make you happy. If not, it is counterproductive to your existence.

This, of course, leads us to the third fundamental value:

Self-Esteem . . .

A sane person accepts him or herself, and is comfortable in his or her own skin. <u>And they are also comfortable with</u>

being selfish, and ensuring that their own needs are met.
They understand that if they were to sacrifice themselves
for others, they would diminish and degrade themselves,
and ultimately be of use to anyone.

Now, this leads us to the next question that arises for many.
Namely, what about love and relationships?

Love is an expression of your self-esteem. And an
expression of your deepest values. You fall in love with
someone who shares these values. And, if you truly do
love someone, it means that they bring happiness to your
life. Or, in other words, *you love them for purely selfish
and personal reasons!*

Because if you weren't in love for this reason, it wouldn't
make sense. If you were in love for a selfless reason, it
would mean that you would get no joy or personal pleasure,
and are there simply for self-sacrificial pity for that person.
That is not love. It is dysfunctional craziness.

That doesn't mean that there are not millions of people who
would accept that kind of sick, superficial love. There are.
But those are the people who want to remain sick, broke,
and stupid. They merely want to suck the joy, life and
energy from your body. Then, when you are as lifeless as
they are, they will be content to know that you share an
equal misery.

In true prosperity, you choose the person you love, and you
fall in love with them because they bring happiness to your
life. This is the highest compliment and honor you can ever
pay another human being—that you love them for the
selfish reason of the happiness and joy they bring you.
Now all of this is not to be confused with Hedonism . . .

The philosophy of Hedonism holds that only what is pleasant or has pleasant consequences is intrinsically good.   The psychology of Hedonism holds that all behavior is motivated by the desire for pleasure and the avoidance of pain. This would seem to suggest that pleasure is a standard for morality. Which is most certainly not the case .. .

That would mean that whatever values you have would be moral. It wouldn't matter if you chose them consciously or subconsciously, with reason, or by emotion. You would be basing your morality on whims, urges, or whatever desires possessed you at the moment. This is definitely immoral. Good must be defined by a rational standard of value. Pleasure is not a "first cause," but rather a consequence. The consequence of actions you take because you have made a rational value judgment.

Let's continue with this logical exploration of this philosophy to live life by. At this stage, many people will ask about serving others and giving to charity. They wonder if I mean that they shouldn't help others or support charities. Glad you asked.

There is this belief that you have a moral obligation to help those less fortunate than you. Nothing could be further from the truth. This is the kind of belief that keeps people sick, broke and stupid.

If you live your life by the principles we are discussing, you very well may help others and contribute to charity. I already told you that my number one expense on my tax return for the last five years or so has been charity. In addition to that, I have often helped others with support, even though no one else knows of it, and I don't get a tax credit.

But here are the three criteria I use:

1) The person or organization is worthy of the support.
2) I can afford to do it.
3) It brings me happiness to do it.

That alone is what determines on where and on whom I spend my charity dollars. It certainly has nothing to do with who is the "neediest," or what causes are politically correct.

I support a great number of causes. The Opera, symphony, my church, wildlife funds, disease prevention and cures, homeless shelters, runaway shelters, and scholarships. I have bought business items and computers for aspiring speakers, performance costumes for upcoming singers, financed martial arts training for foster kids, funded academic scholarships, sponsored more amateur sports teams than I can count, and bought holiday presents for a whole bunch of kids who otherwise wouldn't have received any.

But I did this for purely selfish reasons! For the happiness it brings me. Take the concept even further . . .

You might even step in the way of a bullet that was headed for your spouse or someone you love greatly. If their value to you were so great, that you would not care to live without them, it wouldn't be self-sacrifice. It would be a case of protecting what you value.

And that is where this all leads to. You know exactly what brings value to you, and furthers your purpose, which is a life of happiness. It means accepting that you are supposed to be happy and working towards that end, without guilt. Rejecting the tribal thought surrounding you and refusing to give in to guilt rackets that are practiced on you.

As you look around the world today, it is easy to view man as a helpless, subservient robot. Most people are just worker drones in the collective, living their sick, broke and stupid lives. We are surrounded by mediocrity, depravity and fear. But if you look a little deeper, you'll see something else . . .

You'll see Concorde flying at Mach 2.2, study missions to Mars, and the Golden Gate Bridge. You'll experience a Puccini Opera; read a Hemingway book; or watch Michael Jordan defy the laws of gravity. You'll marvel at the Great Pyramids, the tenacity of Lance Armstrong, or the courage of a single mother battling cancer.

You'll start to see the enormity of the human spirit, and the greatness we are capable of. You'll realize that man is not inherently weak and helpless; he just becomes that way when he refuses to use his rational mind.

And you'll recognize that you yourself can do great things, and do them for the right reasons. You can be bold, daring and imaginative, and leave this world a better place because you were walking on it for a while. When you live your life by the core values of purpose, reason and self-esteem.

Chapter Six
The Prosperity People in Your Life

We have talked about the effect negative people in your
life can have on you. But what about the positive ones?
And what kinds of people do you need to really accept
your abundance in all areas?

I can still remember a pattern I saw over and over again
when I went through group therapy. Someone in the
group would really be bugging me. I would speak up and
say something like, "You know what your problem is?
It's you always (fill in the issue)." The person would, of
course, deny it.

The group would then converge on that person to let him
or her know they were in denial and that what I said was
true. After enough input from enough people, the person
would eventually accept that the issue in question was
one they needed to work on. Then, invariably, someone
would turn to me and say something like...

"Well Randy, that's interesting that you would notice that
in Brian. Because you have exactly the same problem."

I of course, was incredulous, and would immediately let
the person know how off-base they were. I would turn to
the group for support. One look at their eyes would let
me know I was in trouble . . .

They would be eyeing me up like a priest who spots a
fresh crop of altar boys. This was their chance to put
me in my place, and they would hit me with both barrels.

One by one, they would take turns verbally confronting
me on my behavior. They did this for two reasons:

Reason number one was because they hated me. I was arrogant, opinionated and argumentative. I resented the group; I hated being analyzed; and I was in deep denial about my emotional issues. Which is the second reason the group often ganged up on me . . .

Because they were right.

So the argument would last for two or three of the weekly sessions. The group confronting me—me denying it.

I would leave the sessions incensed at the unfairness of it all. Usually, after hours of turning it over in my mind, I would come to the realization that the group was right. Then, I'd have to go back and admit if to them the next session, which pissed me off even more!

And time after time, <u>the whole issue was brought out because I recognized and hated the behavior in someone else</u>. They were the mirror image I needed to start the process.

My pattern was:

- Notice the problem in someone else.
- Confront them.
- Get confronted back.
- Argue and deny.
- Self-searching and deliberation.
- Acceptance and the ability to then move on.

This was a pretty stupid, dysfunctional way to learn lessons, but it was the only one that worked for me at the stage of consciousness I was at. I think this is a common pattern for people who begin the self-development process. It ain't fun, but it works.

So what about you?

What is the process you use for learning, confronting, and changing dysfunctional behavior in your life? How do you recognize and correct personal issues that can be keeping you from happiness and prosperity?

In my case, I've learned how to streamline the process. I now have two ways that I make change.

Process one. I take note when something someone else does really bothers me. I've realized that when something bothers me from another—that may be an issue I need to look at in myself. So the process here is:

- Notice a problem in someone else.
- Self-searching and deliberation.
- Acceptance and the ability to then move on.

The other way this happens for me is when I am confronted by someone I trust. There are only a few of these people in my life. But I trust them explicitly. They have demonstrated to me that they know how to be "real," they are well adjusted, and their own life is working well. They won't tell me what I want to hear, and they're not afraid to "call me on my stuff." So the process here is:

- Someone I trust "calls me on my stuff".
- Self-searching and deliberation.
- Acceptance and the ability to then move on.

Now this doesn't mean that every time I react to someone's behavior, or someone brings my own behavior to my attention—that I automatically accept that I need to change.

Sometimes I'm reacting in a knee-jerk response mode to an old issue I had before. At other times, someone who brings something to me is only projecting his or her own insecurity on me. But I have found that *most* of the time, it is something that I need to address. And when something is brought to me that I'm just not sure about—I will check it out with someone else I trust.

So where does the problem come in?

Finding enough people at the consciousness level I am at. And that is the real issue for you, as well. Because it can be a little daunting to locate these people—and a little scary to let go of the others.

Once you get on the pathway of personal development – you can start to leave people behind real quick. And it's not them you have to worry about – it's <u>you</u>.

Because you may self-sabotage yourself to keep things comfortable . . .

Many of the participants in my coaching program are starting to realize that they are challenged with lack and limitation thinking. They're surrounded with negative people. They might be married to one.

They start to see that moving forward to success is going to mean some change, disruption, and uneasiness. This can cause anxiety that percolates below the surface.

And that could just cause you to not take an action that would move you forward . . .

You might just get into a traffic accident and miss your child custody hearing. You could oversleep and decide not to attend that educational seminar. You might run out of gas and miss that interview for a better job. You might wait a little too long to leave for your appointment, so you take a shortcut through a bad neighborhood, and end up on the wrong end of a gun. You could manifest a drama that keeps you in chaos—and prevents you from meeting the mate that is perfect for you.

Of course you wouldn't intentionally get robbed, get into a car accident or miss a good job. **But people manifest these kinds of things subconsciously every day.**

So how do we really let go of lack? And break patterns that have often been practiced over our entire lifetime?

The reality is, when you are doing the victim thing, as I was, you probably have a very large investment in remaining a victim. And there are probably dozens of little things you do every day to maintain that status.

Let's take being sick as an example. As you know, this was an issue for me. In my case, I was manifesting sickness to get attention, affection, and what I perceived as love. So how does that play out on a daily basis?

Well you probably have four or five people who, whenever they see you, look concerned and ask about your condition. Every time this happens, you get another chance to be a victim.

You may be on medication that allows you to think about your condition three times more a day. You have daily routines, little things you do that are about being sick.

And don't get me started about handicapped parking decals, walkers, wheelchairs and other things like that!

"Now wait a minute," you say. "Surely you are not inferring that I can just throw away my wheelchair, braces, medication, therapy, etc.," you ask.

Well I'm not even going there. I don't need a lawsuit from someone who stops taking their medication, or falls down without their walker. However . . .

I do know that all these things can keep you sick, and being a victim. And I know that sometimes we need them. The real question is when do we really need them, and when are they actually keeping us sick? Think about it.

Now of course those things all have good uses, and we sometimes need them. But, at other times, using them can keep us dependent, and keep us in victim-hood.

Suppose you discover that like me, you've been hanging on to an illness because it gets you attention and affection. You realize this, and vow that tomorrow you will be starting out new, fresh and healthy. But you go to the mall . . .

And there are those handicapped parking spaces, all close to the store and everything. And you're holding on to that decal that allows you to park there . . .

What happens next?

You've got a medicine chest full of pain pills, hospital equipment around the house, or books and articles on your condition. If you become what you think about, what will all that stuff do?

If you have a bunch of friends who continually ask how you are and inquire about your condition, what does that do for your consciousness?

Think about all that. And think about this . . .

We've been using sickness as the example. Think about how you might do something similar In terms of staying broke, missing a promotion, or losing a healthy relationship.

If you're broke right now— and my definition of broke is that you don't have at least $10 million U.S.—how much time do you spend owning being broke? Do you ever repeat the stupid clichés about the rich getting richer, having to have money to make money, etc.? Do you gossip about how cheap your boss or company is?

Have you surrounded yourself with people who wear being poor as a badge of honor? How many of your close friends make a whole lot more than you do? And here's the real big one . . .

Do you spend most of your thoughts about money (worrying about paying bills, where you'll get the money, etc.,) or dreaming of ways to preserve and increase your existing wealth?

So far we've looked at ways we might unwittingly stay sick or broke. Do you think you could do the same thing to threaten a healthy relationship? Or prevent yourself from ever finding one?

Well let me ask . . .

If you're single, do you have a daunting list of qualifications that a prospective candidate must meet in order to qualify? Have you made it next to impossible for a human to qualify?

And if you are coupled, but facing challenge after challenge, is it really all your partner's fault, like you maintain? How many of the negatives in your relationship are exact parallels of the problems you witnessed with your parents?

Guys—does having a "cold, frigid wife," a "bitch ex-wife," or jealous controlling girlfriend (or all three!) fit perfectly into your martyr identity? And ladies, Gays, and anything inbetween—the same questions to you, assuming the appropriate gender bias.

Do you have single friends who get jealous when you are happily seeing someone? What effect might this have on your prospects for a long-term happy relationship?

Do you regale your friends with stories of past injustices from previous relationships? Do you have a "support group" of friends who console you every time you get abused, dumped, or stood up? If so, how much of your identity is tied into this?

In other words, does having unhappy and unhealthy relationships fulfill your vision of yourself as a noble victim? And don't just focus on your spouse, or lack of one. What about your relationships with your family and close friends?

Please spend some time thinking about all this. Perhaps you have decent relationships, but aren't wealthy. Maybe you've got a lot of money, but poor health. Evaluate all the areas of your life, and see if you are subconsciously holding on to victim-hood in any way. It's the first step to limitless abundance!

I was talking to my acupuncturist the other day. We'll call him "Steve." He's a wonderful healer. Trained in China, he really knows his stuff. Yet, I can see that his business is struggling. I also know why . . .

For the past three years I've known him, I have often heard him say things that affirm lack.   And I can tell from his other statements why that is. They come from his underlying beliefs. We both attend the same church. When I ask if he has a lot of clients from church he says things like, "The people that go there are too poor. They're not willing to spend money on things like acupuncture."

I told him that I didn't believe that this particular belief served him. He said, "No it's not a belief. It's a fact. People at that church don't have much money."

"That's not a fact," I said. "Many people at church buy my tapes, attend my seminars, participate in Breakthrough U, and joyfully, gratefully and lovingly spend money with me. There are many prosperous people at that church."

"Ok they spend money for something like you have. But they won't spend money for something like I have. That's just a fact."

He has the belief that people won't spend money for acupuncture. He bases this on the "fact" that his practice has gone down over the last few years, and he knows several other practitioners whose practices have declined.

This is what's known as "confirmation bias." You notice data that supports your prejudice. The reality, of course, is that acupuncture, iridology, massage therapy, homeopathy, and virtually ALL forms of natural and alternative therapies, are exploding across the U.S. and around the world.

He said to me, "A few years ago, I was doing great. I had a big practice in New York, was doing about $120,000 a year, then things started to slide , , ,"

"Wait," I interrupted, "That's problem number one. First of all, doing $120,000 a year is HORRIBLE! That's slave wages for someone with your training and education. So we have to change that belief right now."

"But you don't understand," he said. "In this line of work..."

And then he went on to give me all the reasons to support his limiting beliefs.

I realized that he has the belief that doctors of acupuncture will eke out a living, and struggle to have people accept their services. He sees the profession as a noble chance to serve humanity, but not one that someone can actually make a nice living at. Of course I pointed out that this belief didn't serve him. And of course he pointed out that this wasn't a belief, but a "fact," based his experience of the profession and the people he knows.

This is a very common belief by the way, for many people in the healing professions. And a very foolish one. Any profession that provides great value to people is also one that will make you rich. That's the way that prosperity works.

"How much do you think I'd make a year as an acupuncturist?" I asked Steve.

"Where?" he wanted to know. "In New York?"

"No, not New York. Right here. Actually here, New York, or anywhere," I replied.

He hemmed and hawed, and it was obvious that he didn't want to insult me, but he thought that I would struggle as an acupuncturist as well. I assured him that I would make at least $350,000 to $500,000 a year as an acupuncturist, and at least another two million dollars a year training other acupuncturists how to do the same thing.

Steve simply didn't believe me. The most successful acupuncturist he had ever heard of was one who made $250,000, and that guy wasn't any good, he related.

"So he was a crook?" I wanted to know.

"Well let's just say that he wasn't very ethical," he replied.

Now it was all coming into focus. "So what you're saying is that acupuncturists all struggle to get by, unless they are willing to sell their souls."

At first he resisted, but he slowly came to realize that he did have a core belief that the only way for an acupuncturist to be wealthy was to practice unethically. And that what he considered to be success, would be what I would consider marginally scraping by.

I dug deeper. Turns out he was raised by his grandparents, who were quite poor. He related that he could still hear his grandfather's voice proclaiming—are you ready for this— "We may be poor, but at least we're honest!"

That had been the mantra around the house. Do you have any idea of the effect this kind of programming can have throughout life? When you learn those kinds of lessons at an impressionable age from a trusted parental figure—the effect is quite profound.

It just percolates down there in your subconscious, shaping the beliefs, prejudices, and attitudes you use to form your whole life. It sets up your initial confirmation bias, and the world you see from that point on will be through those tinted glasses.

Not two days after my conversation with Steve, I was chatting with another amazing natural healer, this one a chiropractor who also teaches a unique brand of yoga. He lives for his practice and patients, always learning new techniques, and always striving to treat them in the most holistic and powerful way. He teaches his yoga class on the beach as the sun is setting and the waves are crashing, so it's quite a spectacular experience.

What does he charge for this euphoric healing experience? Seven dollars. Which used to be four or five 'til I beat him up about it last year.

He invited me to his class that night, and jokingly said, "The class is $7, but you can pay $30, so you feel it's worth it."

So of course I chided him for his poverty consciousness pricing. And of course he replied with, "Hey – do you know how many yoga teachers are happy to make $45 a class?"

Which is the equivalent of the convict who says, 'Hey I only killed three people. Charles Manson killed about 20!'

Measuring your worth by the standards of the foolish tribe is very foolish indeed. So I told our yoga-enlightening friend, "But you're not happy unless you make $65 a class, right?"

"No, no, no," he exclaimed. "I made $120 last night."

Now you know what? If he is happy making $120 for a couple hours work, then that's his business. But I think he's capable of a lot more. Just like I think my doctor of acupuncture is.

Now I'm sure both of them would ask the question, "Well Randy, why don't you pay $150 a session for the acupuncture instead of $60, and $30 for the yoga instead of $7?"

Because that would not only be stupid, it would be anti-prosperity. I would be penalizing myself and subsidizing the moochers. I expect to pay the same going rate as everyone else does. And I judge the value I receive by the value that the person providing it sets on it himself or herself.

Now in both these cases, these guys are friends of mine. So I do what I think any good friend does for another. I challenge their prosperity consciousness, and remind them of the greatness they have inside. And point out that the universe rewards greatness with riches – if you are willing to accept it.

So how's your relationship situation? Do you do this role for your friends? Do you have people in your life who will do this for you? And this question . . .

How often do you put yourself in the company of people who challenge your beliefs and expand your concept of what abundance is?

I have lived a life that demonstrates the power of achieving prosperity like few others ever have. I have gone from sickness to abundant health. I have transformed myself from a dishwasher in a pancake house to a multi-millionaire. And I have grown from someone contemplating suicide to living a joyful life of happiness and fulfillment.

That metamorphosis was the result of a number of factors. Changing my beliefs, spending time in daily self-development, learning how the laws of prosperity work, and other things. But the underlying element that drove ALL of these things was that I changed the people in my life.

In my case, I changed where I lived, and where I worked. I stopped hanging out with my victim friends. Now this wasn't done without some discomfort and guilt. Case in point, one night when the telephone rang.

Rackets . . .

Greg was very agitated, and it was obvious in his voice over the phone. "Randy, you say you're a good Christian, but you're always judging me and others. You're so rich now; you forgot what it's like to struggle. You forget that others didn't have the same chances as you. God has blessed you and now you're forgetting about the people less fortunate than you."

I took a deep breath and I smiled to myself. I couldn't help but notice the humor in Greg going back to the well with this old standby again. And why not? It had worked with me many times before.

But not this time . . .

Because this time I had my Star Trek universal translator fired up so even though Greg spoke the words you see above—this is what I heard:

"Randy, I'm going to take your belief in Christianity and use it against you. I have made many foolish decisions, not the least of which is I knocked up a girl, didn't pay child support, called in sick a lot so I got fired from a couple of places, and ran my car into the ground, so it doesn't run. While you were working 70 hours a week, I was just doing enough to get by, so I could watch six hours of television a night and ten hours a day on weekends.

"Now you have things and I don't. Your life is working and mine isn't.

"By talking about Christianity, I'm hoping to manipulate your emotions and make you feel guilty. If I can make you feel guilty enough—you'll 'lend' me another loan, which you and I both know, will never be paid back, just like the last three weren't. By presenting the good decisions, sacrifice and hard work you did as 'luck,' or 'breaks,' I will try to make you feel that life treated me unfairly, and attempt to mooch from you some of what you've earned."

OK, let me level with you. Captain Kirk did not lend me his Universal Translator. I understood what Greg was really saying because I speak fluent "racket-speak."

Now I'm embarrassed to tell you that I know the language so well because I used to be the biggest racketeer of all. And make no mistake—the situation I have just described is a racket. It is the way addicts, parasites and drama queens use you, to bail them out of the bad decisions they have made.

And it usually works!

How can you not feel guilty when you have much, and others have next to nothing? It can be a tough situation; in great part, because of the way the racketeers manipulate you. They are experts at shirking responsibility, and using other factors to manipulate you.

Case in point, Delta Airlines.

On my way back from Singapore, the last leg was a Delta flight from Atlanta to Fort Lauderdale. As usual, they didn't have the paperwork done by departure time, so we were still at the gate twenty minutes later. Then a thunderstorm came in and shut down the airport. So we sat at the gate for over an hour before we could finally leave.

When we finally landed, the pilot thanked us for our patience, and said, "I'm sure you understand. When Mother Nature acts like that, there's not much we can do."

That was a classic racket.

The pilot is pushing off the blame for his and his company's inept performance on the weather. But the truth is, had we taken off on schedule, we would have beaten the storm. But like a lot of racketeers, the crew grabbed at outside circumstances to use them as an excuse to escape responsibility for their own actions.

That's what Greg was doing when he was always wheedling money out of me. This is very common when people are immersed in "victim" behavior. They say something like, "It's not my fault! I couldn't help it. There was an accident on the highway, so traffic was backed up. I was late for the interview and they hired someone else. Then the bank bounced my checks because I was expecting them to give me an advance if they hired me, so I wrote out a few checks because the bills were overdue already, and I . . ."

Sounds good; looks good; looks good on paper. Only problem is, it doesn't work. If that job was so important to your life, you should have left 45 minutes earlier. But victims don't think that way. And when you spend too much time around victims, you start to think like they do.

Don't get me wrong. I would love nothing better than to see Greg and all my other "victim" friends become prosperous. But I can't drag them across the finish line. And you can't do it with your friends either. The best thing you can do is limit your exposure to them when they want to be a victim, and support them when they are wiling to make a real effort to grow their consciousness.

It doesn't serve you to drown in despair with them. Give a man a fish, and you feed him for a day. Teach a man how to fish and he eats for a lifetime. Teach a victim how to fish and he'll sit in a boat and drink beer all day!

Chapter Seven
Religion and Lack

I'm a real enigma to most people. I live my life by objectivist principles, but I believe in a God. I meditate and I drive exotic sports cars. I have a deep connection with my God, but I'm not religious. I preach prosperity, but I'm tough-talking, blunt, and sometimes use language that would make a longshoreman blush.

I have no problem with any of those contrasts, and celebrate them as demonstrations of the rich life I live, the integrity of my message, and the assignment I carry out. I see myself as the prophet of profit, the swami of selfishness, and the minister for the un-ministered. I am never afraid to tell you the truth, as I perceive it. Even when, and especially when, it runs counterculture to accepted beliefs of "the tribe."

About 15 years ago, I had a profound insight on prosperity. I stopped taking financial advice from broke people. I stopped getting health tips from sick people. And I stopped looking for spiritual guidance from people that couldn't demonstrate the manifestation of Universal Laws in their life.

It sounds pretty simple when I write it that way, doesn't it? But I've found that few people can claim to follow this same approach.

It's always the programming that sneaks in the back door that you have to be really concerned with. And of course no one does that back-door programming better than organized religion. Even a lot of people who normally use a lot of discernment in what they allow to permeate their consciousness, often let down their guard when they enter a religious environment.

They mistakenly assume that the content they receive is somehow blessed by God and thus positive for them. Often, it's just the opposite. In fact, when I receive information in a religious setting, I keep my lack radar on Red Alert.

If you can let go of some of the doctrines and dogma that organized religion has programmed you with—you can create a vacuum for spiritual principles to enter your mind. Truth is, the issue here is not about fundamentalism, God, or religion. The ultimate issue here is believing that you are worthy of abundance.

Remember the couple in my Mastermind Retreat that had such a difficult time embracing the idea that could bring them tens of millions of dollars? In their case, I think the cause was their religious beliefs.

Now this is a very common situation in the world today. Organized religion is one of the all-time worst offenders in terms of lack and limitation programming. The Christian church has milked this strategy for centuries, but they are certainly not alone. They have plenty of company.

But this couple had a little different twist.

Of course I told the husband (who is a dear friend of mine, BTW) that I thought they still had an issue accepting prosperity, based on his inability to think what his life would look like if he made $30 million a year. He felt I was way off base, because he is a fundamentalist Christian. And like a lot of fundamentalists, he feels that his religion is a prosperous one.

He is often offended by my attacks on fundamentalism, and he feels that I perceive it as lack programming because so many Christians are enamored with the belief that it is spiritual to be poor. He's right and I do.

He feels that he is not infected with the lack mind virus because he equates believing in Christ, with believing in prosperity. He trotted out all of the usual explanations. God gave his only begotten Son for us, he has a rich heavenly Father who wants Him to have the Kingdom, etc.

That's not the issue, however . . .

Not for him; not for a lot of people. And maybe not for you. I don't see his lack programming coming from the belief that God is withholding things from him, or is not a benevolent provider. (While many fundamentalists have that belief, this is not his problem. He is infected with THE OTHER virus that comes often from organized religions.)

<u>I think the problem he and many other people face is that deep down on a subconscious level, he feels unworthy of those blessings</u>. The problem, as I see it, is not that he doesn't believe in God's love—it is that he feels he is unworthy of that love.

And that is an issue for millions of people. And that is the real crux of what we're talking about here. It's the result of centuries of indoctrination.

By persuading people that it is spiritual to be poor, the religious authorities have maintained power over the masses. They have convinced them that this was the way things were ordained to be. It also has caused people—through fear—to tend to act for the good of the tribe, because anti-social behavior brought the threat of eternal damnation. "If you go against this law, you will be punished in the next life."

Making people fearful of transgressing against the teachings of the priests was therefore a means of controlling them and it also served to keep them meek, docile, satisfied with their lot.

I attended a Sunday morning Christian service at a convention I was attending. The speaker was a layman, who used the opportunity to profess his devotion to God. He was sincere, heartfelt and offered a wonderful, moving message of his faith. I made it a point to introduce myself to him afterward, and let him know what a beautiful job he had done.

A few weeks later, I got a present from him. A book called "The Seeker's Bible." Now I hate to even mention this, because it was a gift given from thoughtfulness, love and brotherhood. But I would just as soon read this thing as stick a fork in my eye. It is absolutely filled with lack and limitation programming. Or at least that's all I can assume, after reading the first few pages of the introduction.

It starts off with the premise—a very common one in religious circles—that happiness on earth is simply not attainable. (BTW, if you think Christians have cornered the market on this belief, check out what some of the Eastern religions teach.)

The book states, "That is why there are so many miserable 'successful' people. How often have we read in the paper about another celebrity checking into a rehab clinic, overdosing on drugs, or committing suicide? Why is that? It's because they 'have it' and know that 'it' just isn't 'it!'"

Of course the subliminal message in statements like the one above is that rich, successful people are unhappy, have addictions and kill themselves. And, of course, we have lots of "proof." John Belushi, Jimi Hendrix, Janis Joplin, Michael Hutchinson, Kurt Cobain, etc., etc.

There is only one problem with this rationale. These things also happen to poor people too. You just don't hear about them.

Yes lots of rich people check into rehab clinics. That's because they can afford them! Have you seen the price of a rehab stay?

Poor people OD and kill themselves every day. In fact, a lot more of them than rich people. You just don't see it on CNN, because most people aren't interested in what happens to some broke bricklayer. "The poor bloke blew his brains out What a shame. Can you pass the mashed potatoes please?"

But if we learn that someone rich and famous blew his brains out—that's good news! Because it feeds our subconscious programming that it is spiritual to be poor, and those rich people are just getting their just desserts.

This Seeker's Bible goes on to talk about people's tendency to want bigger and better. It says, "You would think after earning their first million, people would be satisfied—but it never happens. They make a thousand and they want two thousand. A million, five million. Five million, twenty million—and so on."

It goes on to quote King Solomon, "Just as Death and Destruction are never satisfied, so human desire is never satisfied." And then someone named Joy Davidson, who says, "Living for his own pleasure is the least pleasurable thing a man can do; if his neighbor doesn't kill him in disgust, he will die slowly of boredom and powerlessness."

Now we're getting to the stuff that religion does better than anyone. Guilt!

You have a thousand and you want two thousand? You greedy bugger. You should be ashamed of yourself! Will you never be satisfied?

I could go on for about ten thousand days on this kind of insidious lack programming, but I tire of debating such foolishness. Just know this. Organized religion has been distorting the message of prosperity for centuries. There are enough different quotations in the Bible that you can pull out five of them from various chapters to support just about any opinion you have. And the same thing can be said for the Koran and other religious manifestos. Unless you read these in their entirety, don't bother.

In another quote from "The Seeker's Bible," it says, "The Bible clearly identifies our serious problem as sin. Sin is not just an act but the actual nature of our being. In other words, we are not sinners because we sin. Rather, we sin because we are sinners! We are born with a nature to do wrong . . . We are not basically good—we are basically sinful. This sinfulness spills out into everything we do."

Yeesh! What a belief that is! Now can you imagine how you will feel about yourself —and becoming prosperous— if you are raised believing that? Imagine the subliminal programming of hearing preaching like that over a period of years.

I believe that money is God (or the Universe) in action. There is no separation. Sunshine, and full moons and walks on the beach are spiritual. Good health, happy relationships and love are spiritual too.

But so are financial security, a nice home, beautiful clothes and a car that makes your heart race! Because the only way you get and keep the material things, is by giving a fair exchange of value, and living by the spiritual laws of prosperity.

What would you think if I told you that this continuous desire for more comes from your Spiritual nature—and not from your 'groveling sorry sinner who will rot and burn in Hell with gnashing of teeth' nature? What if I told you that it is "Divine Dissatisfaction" that keeps you growing, developing, and attaining a higher level of consciousness?

Now, if you've been raised in any kind of fundamentalist religion – that's probably the opposite of what you've been programmed with all your life, (BTW, this is pretty much the case in all fundamentalism, from Islamic to Christian, and everything in between. The more you become conscious of this, the easier it is to counter-program against the negativity. And it also means you will become more aware of the self-sabotage it can cause you to do.)

And this is not to say that only having material things will make you happy. It won't. You have to have people you want to share them with. And you must be spiritually grounded. But the point I want you to really get, is that having a desire for these things is not bad—it's Divine! <u>It's what drives you to reach higher and do more, which moves you to a higher level of consciousness!</u>

Now my point in all this is not to get into the individual religions, and I will not debate you on whether your God is the right one or the "real" one. That is not my role, and this is not the place.

And believe it or not, if you don't believe in God, I don't see it as my responsibility to convert you. If you have a belief in natural progression, or universal law, and it is working for you, I celebrate that.

In my experience, atheists and agnostics often have a greater understanding of true spiritual principles than many claiming to be Holy. So it's not you I'm worried about. I believe you will find your path as it unfolds before you. My concern now is those of you who do believe in God . . . I ask you to think about your belief in God. And more importantly your belief in your relationship to God.

Is it fear-based, founded on a belief of a Supernatural being who is making a list and checking it twice, gonna find out who's naughty and nice? Do you see yourself as a sorry sinner who needs to appease your God by groveling and prostrating yourself before Him, to avoid eternal damnation? And if so . . .

Do those beliefs serve you???

What do you think they do to your self-esteem? What do you think they do for your belief in your ability to do great things? How do you think they make you feel about your worth? What do you think those beliefs do for your prosperity consciousness? And will they allow you to accept abundance?

I see the whole concept of "original sin" as a distortion of the Bible. My copy says that God created man in his own image. And He saw everything that He had made, and, behold, it was very good. And as far as I know, He has never changed his mind. So you see I have a belief in "original blessing."

Now you know what? The fundamentalists will argue the point with me all day long. And you know what else? God bless 'em. May the force be with them. They can argue their point all day long with me (and they have), but it doesn't even register on my radar screen. Why?

Because I can see that their beliefs don't serve them. And I have found that my beliefs serve me. So they can quote their scriptures, rub their rosary beads, and hit me upside the head with their eight-pound Bible. My life is working, and I don't believe theirs is.

And that is the issue for YOU. Think about who taught you your beliefs, how long you've had them, and the way they were pushed on you. Ask yourself a very simple question.

Are my beliefs serving me?

God blessed us with free will. And the best way to honor that, and exercise that, is through critical thinking. You probably came to your beliefs on God, religion, and prosperity as a child, based on what religious organization your parents sent you to. Perhaps it is time for some reflective discernment.

Now as I said before, Christianity is not alone in this kind of lack and limitation programming we're discussing. I'm using Christianity as an example here because of the book given me. Now here's what I want you to understand...,

The person who gave me that book did so from a good heart. He even inscribed it to me with the words, "May this copy of God's word offer you hope, encouragement, purpose and peace in Jesus Christ." He has no idea that the book he gave me perpetuates the exact opposite of that!

I'm afraid that like a lot of people, he's heard some things so many times for so long, he has never questioned them with critical thinking. He believes in God; he believes his God is good; yet it never occurred to him that his whole belief system is based upon fear. He has never wondered why a God that is only good would have to be vengeful, punishing, and feared.

If you have been raised in this kind of religious environment, any desires you had for wealth, success and achievement were probably used to make you feel guilty. And you were probably taught that those things wouldn't bring true happiness, but only emptiness, heartbreak and despair.

Now that's certainly an interesting interpretation of desire. I have an entirely different one . . .

I believe the desires we have come from God. They are the vehicles He gives us for spiritual development on this plane. I have a hard time believing that it serves you or God, for you to be broke, unhealthy and unhappy.

I also don't think it serves your Creator for you to be satisfied with the first job you get at the burger joint as you work your way through grade school. And I don't think it's somehow spiritual to be happy with making a thousand instead of two thousand. In fact—I think it is the exact opposite of spiritual!

I think not doing the very best of which you are capable of disrespects your Creator, and the potential you were blessed with. I believe that when you have a desire for something more, it is God knocking on your door, inviting you to do more, have more, and become more.

I see your true spiritual path as evolving and growing, never stopping, always moving toward a higher consciousness, toward your highest good.

About Randy Gage

For more than 15 years, Randy Gage has been helping people transform self-limiting beliefs into self-fulfilling breakthroughs to achieve their dreams. Randy's story of rising from a jail cell as a teen, to a self-made millionaire, has inspired millions around the world.

This compelling journey of triumph over fear, self-doubt, and addiction, uniquely qualifies him as an undisputed expert in the arena of peak performance and extraordinary human achievement. His story and the way he shares it, demonstrate the true power of the mind over outside circumstances.

Randy Gage is a modern day explorer in the field of body-mind development and personal growth. He is the author of many best-selling albums including, *Dynamic Development* and *Prosperity* and is the director of www.BreakthroughU.com.

People from around the world interact and receive personal coaching from Randy through "Breakthrough U", his online coaching and success program. As Dean of BreakthroughU.com, Randy provides insight into how to overcome fear, doubt and self-sabotage to reach success and achieve the highest level of human potential.

For more resources and to subscribe to Randy's free ezine newsletters, visit www.RandyGage.com.

101 Keys to Your Prosperity

"Insights on health, happiness and abundance in your life."

You are meant to be healthy, happy and prosperous. Once you recognize and accept this, it is simply a case of learning the principles that abundance is based on.

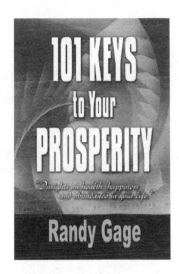

In this insightful book, Randy Gage reveals 101 keys to manifesting that prosperity in your own life. You will move from lack consciousness to living in the light of true abundance. You'll discover:

- What creates prosperity consciousness;
- The universal laws that govern prosperity;
- Why you should embrace critical thinking;
- The secret to creating a vacuum for good; and,
- What it takes to manifest prosperity on the physical plane.

Order the print book or downloadable eBook online at www.Prosperity-Insights.com

Quantity pricing for paperback book:

1–9 books	$7.00 each
10–99 books	$6.00 each
100–499 books	$5.00 each
500–999 books	$4.00 each
1,000 + books	$3.00 each

Accept Your Abundance!
Why You are Supposed to Be Wealthy

"Claim the Prosperity That is Your Birthright."

Do you believe that it is somehow spiritual to be poor? One reading of this fascinating book will dissuade you of that belief fast. You'll understand that you are meant to be healthy, happy and wealthy.

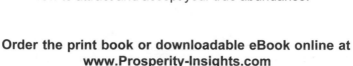

Prosperity guru Randy Gage cuts through the religious dogmas to reveal why becoming rich is your spiritual destiny. You'll discover:

- Why poverty is a sin;
- What may be keeping you from your prosperity;
- Why being wealthy is your natural state;
- The difference between the way rich and poor people think; and,
- How to attract and accept your true abundance!

Order the print book or downloadable eBook online at
www.Prosperity-Insights.com

Quantity pricing for paperback book:

1–9 books	$7.00 each
10–99 books	$6.00 each
100–499 books	$5.00 each
500–999 books	$4.00 each
1,000 + books	$3.00 each

37 Secrets About Prosperity

"A revealing look at how you manifest wealth."

In this landmark book, prosperity guru Randy Gage unveils 37 little-known insights into the science of prosperity. Gage breaks it down into simple, understandable explanations, so you can apply the information in your life immediately to create your own prosperity. He reveals how he went from a dishwasher in a pancake house to a self-made multi-millionaire.

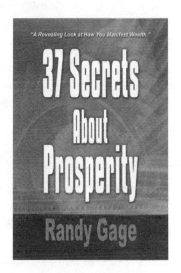

You'll learn:

- Why most people remain poor;
- How the rich leverage their prosperity;
- Why you should emulate certain business models;
- What separates broke, sick and unhappy people from the rich, healthy and happy ones; and,
- How you can manifest prosperity in all areas of your life.

Order the print book or downloadable eBook online at www.Prosperity-Insights.com

Quantity pricing for paperback book:

1–9 books	$7.00 each
10–99 books	$6.00 each
100–499 books	$5.00 each
500–999 books	$4.00 each
1,000 + books	$3.00 each

Prosperity Mind!

How to Harness the Power of Thought

"Brilliant Insights on health, happiness and abundance in your life."

Since "Think and Grow Rich" people have been fascinated with the power of the mind to accomplish great things. Now a recognized expert in human potential cracks the code on how you program yourself for prosperity!

In this breakthrough book, prosperity guru Randy Gage reveals how you can actually program your subconscious mind to move from lack consciousness to prosperity thought. In it, you'll discover:

- How to identify self-limiting beliefs that hold you back;
- The 5 common expressions you probably use every day, which program you for failure on a subconscious level;
- How to practice the "vacuum law" of prosperity to attract good in your life;
- Imaging techniques to manifest things you want; and,
- How you can actually program your own subconscious mind for riches!

Order the print book or downloadable eBook online at www.Prosperity-Insights.com

Quantity Pricing for paperback book:

1–9 books	$7.00 each
10–99 books	$6.00 each
100–499 books	$5.00 each
500–999 books	$4.00 each
1,000 + books	$3.00 each

The 7 Spiritual Laws of Prosperity

"Live your life by the universal laws that govern health, happiness and abundance."

It is your birthright to be healthy, happy and prosperous. Accept this truth and it's simply a case of learning and living by the 7 Spiritual Laws that govern abundance.

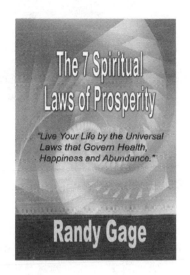

In this breakthrough and insightful book, Randy Gage reveals the secrets behind harnessing these laws to manifest your own prosperity. You'll learn about each of these Prosperity Laws and discover how to:

- Create a vacuum for good;
- Use imaging to get what you want;
- Find and keep your perfect soul mate;
- Use creativity to get the bills paid; and,
- Attract money, health and harmony to your life.

Order the print book or downloadable eBook online at www.Prosperity-Insights.com

Quantity pricing for paperback book:

1–9 books	$7.00 each
10–99 books	$6.00 each
100–499 books	$5.00 each
500–999 books	$4.00 each
1,000 + books	$3.00 each

Order Online at **www.Prosperity-Insights.com**
or call 1-800-432-4243 or (316) 942-1111

The Prosperity Series
by Randy Gage

You are meant to be healthy, happy and prosperous. Once you recognize and accept this, it is simply a case of learning the principles that abundance is based on.

In this insightful series, you will move from lack consciousness to living in the light of true abundance.

Randy Gage reveals . . .

- What creates prosperity consciousness;
- The universal laws that govern prosperity;
- Why you should embrace critical thinking;
- The secret of creating a vacuum for good;
- What it takes to manifest prosperity on the physical plane; and,
- Why you are supposed to be wealthy.

Get all five books now and start living a life of abundance!

Order The Prosperity Series by Randy Gage online:

www.Prosperity-Insights.com

The Prosperity Series, 5 print books $30
The Prosperity Series, 5 eBooks $20
The Prosperity Series, all 5 print books and eBooks
Combination Special $47

Prosperity:
How to Apply Spiritual Laws to Create Health, Wealth and Abundance in Your Life
by Randy Gage

This album will help you uncover the subconscious "lack" programming you have that is holding you back. Then, you'll replace it with prosperity consciousness to manifest money, health, great relationships, happiness, and strong spiritual harmony.

True prosperity comes from understanding and living by the spiritual laws that govern our world. This album takes you through each of the Seven Spiritual Laws that govern prosperity and shows you how to apply them. You will discover the ancient secrets to manifest prosperity in your own life.

You'll discover:

- Why you're supposed to be rich;
- The secrets of optimum health;
- How to get out of debt;
- The Seven Spiritual Laws you must live by;
- Your special powers for prosperity; and,
- How to image—then manifest—boundless, limitless prosperity.

This album will take you on a journey of spiritual enlightenment. You'll learn the practical applications so you can manifest prosperity in your life NOW! You'll learn about faith, the principle of attraction, and even how to use creativity to get the bills paid! This is the most specific, detailed and comprehensive album ever produced on how to become prosperous. **Don't you need it now?**

Prosperity: 8 CDs–2 volume album #A28CD $107
Prosperity: 8 audio-tape album #A28 $97

Dynamic Development
Achieve Your True Potential with the Dynamic Development Series
by Randy Gage

Do you live a life of joy—or simply get through the week? Can you communicate well with your family and co-workers, or do you struggle to be heard? Are you in open, honest and loving relationships, or do you hide behind a mask? How much more can you earn, learn, love and accomplish? *If you want to break out of self-imposed limitations and break through to your true potential—the* **Dynamic Development Series** *is the perfect resource for you.*

Instantly hailed when it was released as the ultimate self-development resource, this is a two-year program to nurture your personal growth and achieve your innate greatness. Each month you will receive an audiotape from human achievement expert Randy Gage with a lesson, and some "homework" to complete that month.

It's a continuing journey on your path of personal development. Each month will bring you on an in-depth study in some area of human achievement, whether body, mind or soul. You'll discover new truths about yourself and uncover old ones. You'll desire more, obtain more, and accomplish more . . . by becoming more.

Dynamic Development, Volume 1, 12 audio-tapes
#V2 $147

Dynamic Development, Volume 2, 12 audio-tapes
V4 $147

BEST DEAL! Both Dynamic Development Volumes,
24 audio-tapes #V2V4S $247

Crafting Your Vision

Twelve success experts share their secrets to success . . .

As soon as this 12 audiotape album was released, it was hailed as one of the greatest self-development tools since *Think and Grow Rich!* It gets to the real root cause of success or failure—the vision you create for yourself.

It's pleasing to your ego to assume your prosperity is not growing because of outside factors and other circumstances. **But the truth is—you are reaping the results of the vision you created!**

Your suffering, frustration or failure to reach goals is the result of a neutral or negative vision—just as the blessings in your life are the results of a positive vision. This is an immutable, unshakable universal law. Living the lifestyle of your dreams begins with crafting the vision of where you want to go. For without a clear, compelling vision you simply cannot achieve what you're truly capable of. And there simply is no better resource to help you create an empowering vision for yourself than this amazing resource.

You'll learn how to craft your personal vision, how to design a vision big enough to encompass the visions of your people, and the steps to take on a daily basis to bring your vision to reality. You'll hear 12 complete programs on vision—recorded live—from 12 of the foremost experts on direct selling, recruiting and marketing.

This breakthrough album includes talks by:

Richard Brooke	Michael S. Clouse	Rita Davenport
John Milton Fogg	Matthew Freese	Randy Gage
Lisa Jimenez, M.Ed.	John Kalench	John David Mann
Jan Ruhe	Tom Schreiter	Tom Welch

When you finish, you'll really know how to craft and manifest the vision of where you want to go. Make sure this resource is in your personal development library. **Get it today!**

Crafting Your Vision–12 audio-tape album #A30 $97

Get Randy Gage As

The only ongoing education program specifically designed for your success! Get personal, individualized success coaching from **Randy Gage**. Join Randy as he helps you expand your vision, shatter self-doubt, and reach your true success potential. Breakthrough U is your opportunity to have Randy as your personal success coach—mentoring you through the mindset, consciousness, and daily actions necessary to reach the success you are capable of.

Initiate Level

This is level one of an amazing journey of self-discovery. Each day you will receive a "Daily Awakening" e-mail message filled with mind-expanding exercises and success lessons to teach you how to think like ultra-successful people think. In addition to these "mind aerobics," you'll receive marketing tips, prosperity secrets and just general success information on how to make it to the top.

You will also have access to the members-only forum on the site so that you can network with other success-minded individuals, and get an invitation to attend Randy's Breakthrough U Success Events.

This is priced inexpensively and is for the beginning success seeker. If you've faced adversity, are deeply in debt, maxed out on your credit cards, or simply starting the journey—this is the program for you. Randy created this level so that those who are down and out— but committed to getting "up and in" —have a vehicle to do so. It's a program to change your consciousness, one day at a time.

Now, if you are further along the path, and serious about reaching higher levels of success—you're ready to advance to...

Alchemist Level

Alchemy, if you'll remember, is the medieval philosophy of transmutation: converting base metals to gold. This is the level for you if you're seeking a transmutation in your life: converting base thoughts and desires into the thinking and actions that produce rich and prosperous outcomes.

(continued on the next page)

Order Online at **www.RandyGage.com**
or call 1-800-432-4243 or (316) 942-1111

Your Personal Coach!

Like the Initiate Level, you will receive the Daily Awakening messages, access to the members-only forum, and an invitation to Randy's Success Convention. You will also receive:

- The "Alchemy Transmutation Kit" (with intro lesson, CDs and binder);
- A subscription to the monthly lessons;
- Access to the monthly online video seminars;
- Monthly Tele-seminars
- Two Personalized Consultations

Now, if you're serious as a heart attack about success, and want to get even more individualized and personal coaching . . . you might want to consider the pinnacle level:

Mastermind Council

This is Randy's "inner circle" of select consulting clients, business partners, and colleagues. They receive a package of benefits so lucrative, that it's never been offered anywhere before. Membership in the **Mastermind Council** gives you a chance to get the most personalized help and guidance from Randy individually—as well as interacting with some of the brightest entrepreneurial minds on the planet.

In addition to the same benefits as the Alchemist, you will also receive:

- Ten Personalized Consultations;
- The chance to participate in twelve live Mastermind Conference Calls a year;
- Members-only Council Updates; and,
- The chance to participate in the Mastermind Retreatseach year.

For complete details go to:
www.BreakthroughU.com

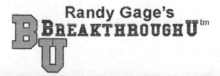

Randy Gage's
BREAKTHROUGHU™

The Midas Mentality:
Expecting and Accepting Your Abundance

This program is the first resource of its kind, ever developed in the world. It will transform you from lack and limitation programming to prosperity consciousness. For 31 days, Randy Gage will work with you, helping you go through the same transformation that he did. He will help you peel away limiting beliefs and replace them with beliefs that serve you and he will help you identify fears and conquer them.

And level upon level, he will guide you in a metamorphosis of your thought process—from how sick, unhappy and broke people think—to the way healthy, happy, rich people do.

30 Audio CDs, 2 DVDs, Study Guide & Randy Jr. CDRom

It is a multi-media format, scientifically developed to literally change the way you think. You will create new neural pathways in your brain, develop your critical thinking skills, and foster whole brain synchronicity between the two hemispheres of your brain.

You will develop the multi-millionaire's mindset, which is the first—and most critical—step to becoming open.

On day one, you'll watch the DVD entitled, "The Science of Manifesting Prosperity." Then you'll load the CD-ROM into your computer. This will cause the "Randy Jr" character to pop up on your computer screen once each day, giving you one of his 101 keys to prosperity.

Then on the next day, you'll start the first of 30 daily lessons on audio CD. You listen to each lesson, then go to your workbook and complete the day's task. On average, this will take you from 45 minutes an hour per day. Do only one lesson each day, to ensure that it "sets," and you are at a different consciousness when you start the next day's lesson.

Following the thirty CDs and workbook lessons, you then watch the final DVD, "Putting Your Prosperity in Place." Of course the "Randy Jr." character will keep popping up everyday, to keep your thoughts on track.

Trust me when I tell you that you will be thinking entirely different than when you started. You will have the mindset of a multi-millionaire, the single most important step to becoming one. You see, you can't be treated for prosperity; you can only be open to receiving it. By the time you finish this program, you will be. Really.

The Midas Mentality–30 audio CDs, 2 DVDs, Study Guide & Randy Jr. CDRom $997

Order Online at **www.ProsperityUniverse.com**
or call 1-800-432-4243 or (316) 942-1111

Randy Gage's Recommended Resources	Price	Qty	Total
Prosperity by Randy Gage Select: ¨ audiotapes or ¨ CD's	$97 (tapes) $107 (CDs)		
The Midas Mentality 30 day prosperity program	$997		
Dynamic Development Series Volume One by Randy Gage	$147		
Crafting Your Vision 12 audiotape album	$97		
Prosperity Series 5 books	$30		
101 Keys to Your Prosperity book	$7		
The 7 Spiritual Laws of Prosperity book	$7		
Prosperity Mind! book	$7		
Accept Your Abundance! book	$7		
37 Secrets About Prosperity book	$7		

United Parcel Shipping Table Order Total 2-Day Ground $50.00 or under $11.60 $5.50 $50.01-$250.00 $13.20 $6.00 $250.01-over $16.20 $7.00 For Alaska, Hawaii, and Canada - regular shipping cost, and add 10%. For foreign and overseas orders, figure the total of your order, plus the regular shipping cost, and add 20%	Subtotal $_____ Shipping (see chart) $_____
Terms: 60-day money back guarantee! Contact us within 60 days of your invoice date if, for any reason, you're not 100% satisfied with any product you've received from us. Product must be in re-sellable condition. Customer Service: 1-800-946-7804 or (316) 942-1111	$_____ **TOTAL**

PAYMENT TYPE: ¨ Visa ¨ MC ¨ AMEX ¨ Discover or
               ¨ Cash ¨ Check

Please print clearly
Credit Card # _ _ _ _ _ _ _ _ _ _ _ _ _ _ _ _

Expires: (MM/YY) ____/____ Signature:_____

Full Name:

Address: Apt./Suite#

City: State: Zip: Country:

Phone: Email:

Ordering & Customer Service: Prime Concepts Group Inc.
1807 S. Eisenhower St. • Wichita, Kansas 67209-2810 USA
1-800-432-4243 or (316) 942-1111 • Fax: (316) 942-5313
www.ProsperityUniverse.com